OUT FROM HIDING!

Also by Dell F. Sanchez...

In English

The Last Exodus

Sephardic Destiny–A Latino Quest

Aliyah! The Exodus Continues

Obadiah–The despised prophet of Sephardim

In Spanish

El Ultimo Exodo

Destino del Sefardim–la busqueda del Latino

Alia–El Exodo Continua

Abdias–El profeta despreciado del Sefardim

In German

Das Geheimnis von Sepharad

Other resources

All these books along with a host of professionally produced DVD teachings on the history and destiny of Sephardic Anusim can be found at www.4sephardim.com.

OUT FROM HIDING!

—Evidences of Sephardic Roots among Latinos—

Dell F. Sanchez, Ph.D.

iUniverse, Inc.
New York Bloomington

Out From Hiding!
Evidences of Sephardic Roots among Latinos

Copyright © 2010 by Dell F. Sanchez, Ph.D.

All rights reserved. No part of this book may be used or reproduced by any means, graphic, electronic, or mechanical, including photocopying, recording, taping or by any information storage retrieval system without the written permission of the publisher except in the case of brief quotations embodied in critical articles and reviews.

iUniverse books may be ordered through booksellers or by contacting:

iUniverse
1663 Liberty Drive
Bloomington, IN 47403
www.iuniverse.com
1-800-Authors (1-800-288-4677)

Because of the dynamic nature of the Internet, any Web addresses or links contained in this book may have changed since publication and may no longer be valid. The views expressed in this work are solely those of the author and do not necessarily reflect the views of the publisher, and the publisher hereby disclaims any responsibility for them.

ISBN: 978-1-4502-5371-0 (sc)
ISBN: 978-1-4502-5373-4 (ebook)
ISBN: 978-1-4502-5372-7 (dj)

Library of Congress Control Number: 2010912554

Printed in the United States of America

iUniverse rev. date: 9/28/2010

—Unrolling the scroll of remembrance—
Malachi 3:16

Dedication

To my wife—my best friend

To Sephardic Anusim pioneers who desire to make

the Negev their home

Coming out of hiding is like a tiny star between worlds!

List of Illustrations

Small box with gold Star of David (left) and Mezuzah inside box (right)	18
Gravestone with Hebrew & Spanish inscriptions	20
Gravestone of Trinidad V. Gonzalez	21
Isaac Morfin's gravestone	22
Photo of structure of old San Felipe Church	23
Inside San Felipe Church with Stars of David over altar	24
Structure of St. Francis Catholic Cathedral	25
Arch with Hebrew letters atop St. Francis Catholic Cathedral	25
Virgin Mary Painting	27
Decalogue Stone & Dell Sanchez on Hidden Mountain	29
Photo of actual structure	32
Combento Sn Diego	32
Photo of pillar and description of Inquisition	33
The Garrote	35
Iron Masks	36
Wheel with Skeleton	37
The Pear Torture tool	38
Bar graph #1 of the International Sephardim DNA Chart	43
Bar graph #2 of the Santa Fe DNA Chart	45
Bar graph #3 of the 4Sephardim DNA Chart	47
Juan Ancira (left) and Fidel Martinez	62
Rachel Garcia	65
Bernadette Martinez	70
William E. Sanchez (left) and Dell F. Sanchez	76
Arnella Martinez with Husband Orlando	82
Kathy Baca	93
Moses Orona	98
Cari Gillespi (right) and Daughter	103
Tatiana Barrera Guzman	107
Jesse Gonzalez	111

Javier Gonzales	114
Arlene Iacone	118
Joseph S. Berrios	121
Leticia Soto	124
Francisco Javier Lizarraga Lopez	127

Preface

The awakening of Sephardic Anusim among Latinos has been a glorious one. It has opened new pathways of expression for them to reconnect with their Jewish roots and revealed their true identity. However, they are soon discovering that these pathways are a long and sometimes treacherous journey back to the original families they were severed from over five hundred years ago.

The minority of these families have managed to preserve some form of recognition regarding their Sephardic Jewish ancestry through many generations. However, the overwhelming majority is barely aware of the fact that their ancestors were Jews of Spain. By way of definition, these Jews of Spain are known as Sephardic Jews or Sephardim. They have also been called *Marranos*, meaning swine or pigs because they were forced to convert to Roman Catholicism by the Spanish Inquisition, then forced to eat pork and called *Marranos* there after. They were also known as *Conversos* and *Nuevos Creyentes* meaning "converts" or "new believers." In recent times, they are also referred to as *Anusim* or *B'nei Anusim* which speaks of the manner in which their ancestors were coerced to convert, which smacks of racially being raped. All in all, the Inquisition was Spain's method of executing its own pogrom or holocaust. Chapter two of this book explains in more detail these facts.

Today, most of them begin this long journey excited and intrigued by the prospects of their new discoveries and by being reconnected with their true family. However, they soon discover that this journey is fraught with unexpected oppositions which make it seem even longer. They often experience rejection by those being left behind and also by those they are moving toward. Many feel as if they are between worlds.

In the middle of their life changing journey, they discover that there is much more than history, genealogy, DNA, and a host of secret stories to their new found life. They experience the rude awakening of something way deeper. They find out that there is a distinct philosophy of life that is quite different to the one they were raised in. This philosophy of life translates itself into radically different expressions of their personal faith and beliefs. Unprepared for it, they discover the inevitable reality that this journey is highly impacted with an array of religious beliefs which they will need to carefully manage depending on how they wish to proceed.

What makes it harder is when they begin to see the duplicity and hypocrisy in this new journey which very few are able to endure. On the one hand they begin to taste the bitterness of being criticized and at times ostracized from old Christian circles, including what on the surface appear to be true Zionists. Later they discover certain pockets of pseudo Christians, and pseudo Jews that get very upset if they don't join their circles. Finally, they discover a major schism between where they are coming from and where they think they are going. They are confronted with the reality of 'how Jewish they intend to be.' So now they find that they must make a decision that will make some people happy and others very upset because of their new persuasion, even if they themselves are thrilled about the new direction in their life.

On top of all of this they become aware that reconnecting with the very land of their forefathers (Israel) isn't quite as easy as they thought it would be. For those traveling to Israel with aspirations beyond that of a tourist, they quickly discover that the Israeli family is enigmatic as some are very religious, yet the majority is not. As they tread the narrow pathway known as *Aliyah* in their longing to become one with the land and the people of their ancestry, they soon discover the politics of becoming an Israeli citizen. They are faced with the harshest reality in this quest when they realize they must jump over many hurdles in order to simply reconnect with the family of their true ancestry. In the interim, they quickly discover that the hurdles keep getting higher and closer with very little definition on how to successfully achieve one's connection with the life they long to belong to.

By the time a Sephardic Anusim family or individual arrives at this hurdle-jumping exercise, they are often too exhausted in spirit and sometimes too broke and broken to continue fighting every step of an uphill battle. Meantime, they learn they must watch their back against those left behind and having to be ever watchful for ambushes set by those that really want nothing to do with their ascent to the land of their forefathers. "But why?" they ask. This is simply because they are different by the decisions their fleeing ancestors had to make in order to survive impending annihilations strewn all across their histories.

I am fully aware that despite all the evidences which this book provides, some Christians as well as Jews will continue to reject these descendants of the survivors who overcame Inquisitions, pogroms and holocausts which took place many centuries ago but feel as if it happened during their parents' generation.

I need to state that this book is not a manual for those desiring to endure this long and treacherous journey. However, it is intended to provide some vital evidences that prove the existence of Sephardic Anusim among a people with a Hispanic/Latino background in America. This book intends to shut the mouths of cynics or at least to quiet them down long enough to prove their existence.

I would be remiss if I would not declare that there are a few wonderful people that happen to be Jewish who have taken a few Sephardic Anusim under their wings in order to help them along the way. Some of these Jews are amazing rabbis and leaders both in America as well as in Israel. Even though some of them have put their reputation on the line, we have discovered that there continues to be a few influential rabbis and

Israeli leaders who are bent on helping Sephardic Anusim come back home.

All things being equal, the merits, the significance and value of this long journey are worth traversing. Even though the numbers of Sephardic Latinos on this pathway are few in comparison with their true numbers, they are like sparks in the dark—the darker the dark, the brighter the spark.

Acknowledgements

I desire to acknowledge some very special people in my life. These include Joshua Stampfer, Rabbi Emeritus of the Neveh Shalom Congregation in Portland, Oregon who has been an amazing instrument of inspiration and assistance to me.

I am profoundly indebted to Rabbi Scheinberg, chief rabbi of Rodfei Sholom Synagogue in San Antonio, Texas. Rabbi Scheinberg has been as an angel from heaven to me, my family and my people. Along with him I wish to acknowledge Rabbi Cohen, Rabbi Sunshine, Bobbie Ghitis, and Gina Meishar. All have been incredible inspirations through their instruction and friendship.

Much of what my wife, Helen, and I have accomplished in the Negev would never have been possible without the caring commitment of Shmulik Riffman, Abraham Duvdevani and Dr. Paula Kabalo, who are amazing Israeli leaders and friends.

Table of Contents

Preface	xiii
Acknowledgements	xvii
Introduction	xxi
A note on the locations and sources of investigation	xxv
Overview	xxvii
Chapter One – Scriptural Evidence	1
Torah Precedence	
Prophetic Precedence	
Talmudic Corroboration	
Chapter Two – Historical Evidences	6
Chapter Three – Material Evidences	16
Chapter Four – Scientific Evidences	39
Chapter Five – Onomastic Evidences	53
Chapter Six – Personal Evidences	64
Chapter Seven –Synthesis of Personal Evidences	130
Chapter Eight – Implications and Projections	133
Conclusions	136
Appendix	140
Notes	144
Bibliography	150
About the Author	153

Introduction

This book is not your traditional history book or one based on a narrow, monolithic topic. However, the nuclear core of the book has to do with various imperative elements affecting one central theme. This theme is about today's Sephardic Anusim who are the descendants of Spanish Jews that endured a three hundred year holocaust in Spain and another three hundred years in Mexico. There is a degree of diversity in topic yet with one singular core theme.

My journey began in the spring of 1996 because that is when my father discovered the secret of his family's Jewish ancestry. As the baby of the family, he was the last one to find out at age 77 about his father having been given up for adoption by a military officer in the Mexican Army who happened to be a Jew. According to DNA test results he was of a Uralic speaking ancestry whose forefather either married a Jewish woman or converted to Judaism many generations ago.[1]

In the process of exploring my own lineage, I discovered truths with a much longer historical record and much deeper implications. In the process, I also discovered facts on my father's mother's side who are Sephardic descendants of a popular family in Monterrey, Mexico. And I also discovered facts about my mother's father's DNA that point directly to a Sephardic ancestry as well. Chapter four is devoted to this whole issue on DNA.

The next thing that began to unfold was the long standing story of my wife's maternal Sephardic ancestry which was common knowledge among all their relatives. But it wasn't until her brother took a DNA test when we discovered that her father's DNA was among the most popular ones among Jews today. The irony is that we have not been successful in finding his surname in genealogical records and his oral history was the least known to us all.

His surname, *Ancira*, is among the least common in North America.[2]

All along, my theory was somewhat less selfish than it seemed. When I first began this journey, I was persuaded that if two of us, my wife and I, had such a peculiar ancestry like the one unfolding before our eyes, how many more were out there with similar stories?

But it wasn't until these last few months when I sensed I had gone full circle. After impassionedly investigating and traveling all across the Southwest of the United States, including Mexico and Spain; and making two trips per year to Israel for the last fourteen years, I finally began to see the bigger picture.

The picture has become a gigantic mosaic demonstrating all forms of evidence that point to the fact that I did not lose my direction during this journey's complexities. What seemed like ancient history dating back hundreds of years began to take shape in the form of new and undiscovered frontiers within my quest. I refer to it in this manner because this is how it seemed to me at that point in time. When I started this journey, there didn't seem to be as much attention on this subject as we have today. Today, we have evidence that a significant number of Latinos happen to have deep ancestral Sephardic roots. Invariably, I refer to them as Sephardic Anusim.[3]

Some of these frontiers are ageless, specifically those documented in Holy Scriptures such as the Torah, the Prophets and the Jewish Talmud. Other frontiers have to do with the diversity and the extant of historical records and genealogies which corroborate the intent of this book. When I least expected it, other *senderos* or narrower paths began to open up in the realms of onomastics which is the science, the art and discipline of surnames. Then the field of material evidences opened up such as those being discovered including mezuzahs, gravestones and epigraphy on boulders, buildings and artwork. All along, the new frontier of DNA testing within the context of human ancestries began to slowly open up newer pathways. These paths are exciting because not only do they confirm a person's true lineage but it helps find existing relatives we often do not know of.

So it is that I have gone full circle in my quest to discover true knowledge. But this circle does not end here. In fact, this circle is yet in its infancy. I expect this knowledge will continue to increase and possibly introduce new and uncharted pathways which I shall pursue probably for the rest of my life.

In the process, I would not doubt that as these circles of knowledge and truth continue to expand and intertwine into new relationships, it might all end up in the land of our forefathers which is Erez Israel.

There are six major topics that accentuate the existence and nature of Sephardic Anusim, they are: history which has been documented (both secular as well as sacred); oral history pertaining to thirteen contributors; science as pertaining to DNA outcomes; onomastics as pertaining to the origin of names; material evidences found within the community of Sephardic Anusim; and finally, my personal observations, assessment and conclusions regarding the overall portrait which this book represents.

A note on the locations and sources of investigation

The knowledge and information compiled in this book represent fourteen years of constant inquiry and investigation. The locations of this investigation include but are not limited to public and university libraries as well as archivists and archive centers in Texas, New Mexico, California, Arizona, Mexico as well as Israel. We have reviewed volumes of books and scanned through genealogical records and archives, particularly in the libraries of the Latter Day Saints center in Salt Lake City, Utah. We have also scoured the internet for reliable knowledge and information that is pertinent to our investigation.

Some of the most exciting investigative adventures have been in our journeys to actual locations with a rich history on the Sephardic Anusim in America, Mexico, Spain and Israel. Interviewing some of the experts and developing positive relationships with them has been a most rewarding experience which has often developed into special friendships that last to this day.

A few of these rewarding experiences have been traveling to Israel at least twice a year for the last fourteen years and inquiring of Israeli leaders as well as Jews in the grassroots sector at every level to find out what they know about the Sephardim and those that fled the

Spanish and Portuguese Inquisitions across the Atlantic and into the New World.⁴

In one of the many journeys, I traveled with a professional video cameraman in order to document each step of this investigative odyssey. A most heartening discovery was to find out that so many Israelis actually spoke Spanish or the language of the Sephardim known as *Ladino*. It was amazing to discover how many of these interviewees that we picked off the streets learned their Spanish/Ladino from their own Jewish parents who had made Aliyah from Spain and even Mexico, Latin America, as well as other European and North African countries to where Sephardim had fled. Being able to effectively communicate with them in my mother tongue was a treat I shall never forget. The knowledge I gleaned from this sector of Jewish people was among the most rewarding of them all because finally I began to connect the dots of the other side of the family which our forefathers were severed from over 500 years ago.

Overview

The aim of this book is to provide positive evidences that corroborate the existence of Sephardic Jewish roots among many American Latinos today. The book begins with ancient readings found in the Holy Scriptures as they relate to the general prospect of Jews from around the world returning to the home of their forefathers, Israel. This chapter emphasizes what ancient prophets have to say about this matter and specifically about the Sephardim and major issues surrounding this theme.

The book moves on to a long term historical survey beginning with the origins of Jews in Spain during the biblical kings. It then proceeds with the persecutions and Inquisitions that forced Sephardim to flee across the Atlantic into Mexico and later across the border into the Southwest of the USA. This chapter deals with the successes and challenges they faced as many went underground in their attempt to survive, thus becoming Crypto Jews, or Jews in hiding.

The next chapter discusses what is known as material evidences which include physical objects that tell a story related to the people in question. It studies the matter of gravestones and hidden objects with Hebraic inscriptions. It also looks at the epigraphy or ancient writings on boulders as well as Hebrew signs and letters on physical structures such as cathedrals and churches.

Following is a discussion on scientific evidences in the field of DNA which point directly to the presence of Sephardic DNA haplogroups among Latinos today. It compares two projects in the Southwest with evidences at an international level.

This is followed by a chapter on evidences that pertain to authentic Sephardic surnames. It elaborates on the various subdivisions and categories of surnames that help provide the reader with a comprehensive perspective on what it means to have a Sephardic surname and how they obtained it.

The book closes with a host of oral histories as provided by thirteen contributors who open up their hearts to share personal and family secrets that point directly to their Sephardic Crypto Jewish reality. These stories are varied as some focus on hard core genealogies, or DNA, as well as secret anecdotes, sayings, practices and beliefs.

The intent of this book is to provide a broad base of foundational knowledge that can be built upon in order to corroborate and, indeed, prove the existence of Sephardic roots among Latinos in America.

The book closes with general observations from this author as well as implications and projections on issues that are now arising or soon to arise as Sephardic Anusim or Crypto Jews continue to emerge on a daily basis all across our Americas. These projections and conclusions are hard hitting statements made by this author which portray both a good news–bad news scenario regarding issues and dilemmas that lie ahead for those 'coming out from hiding.'

Chapter One – Scriptural Evidence

The Hebrew Torah has stood the test of time for around 3500 years. It has been the basis and point of departure for various religions for over three millennia. It has also been the subject for inquiry not only in schools of theology but has also been read in the halls of history, literature and human origins.

In this case, there is no better standard, in my opinion, that relates to the existence and future of Sephardic Anusim than that of Holy Scriptures. These Scriptures can be seen as historical or they can be seen strictly as "inspirational." In either case, they provide an ancient reason for Sephardic Anusim's existence as well as their future role in human civilization. My intent is not the theology of the matter but to corroborate the origins and future of the people this book represents.

I shall quote only a few Scriptures which provide us with some precedence on this subject. The Scriptures I shall refer to are taken verbatim from the Massoretic Text of the Scriptures. The Massoretic Text reads like "Old English" and I do so because it is a reliable source for Biblical translation and is also the basis for the Jewish Bible.

Torah Precedence

In the Book of Deuteronomy it reads:

> *If any of thine that are dispersed be in the uttermost parts of heaven, from thence will the LORD thy God gather thee, and from thence will He fetch thee. And the LORD thy God will bring thee into the land which thy fathers possessed, and thou shalt possess it; and He will do thee good, and multiply thee above thy fathers.*[5]

Prior to his death, Moses foretold what would happen to Jews of every tribe and possibly from every age and generation. With accuracy, Moses foretold the future dispersions of the "Chosen People." History has revealed that the Sephardic Anusim have been in hiding the longest and separated the farthest from the rest of the Jewish family since they were expelled from Spain. No other group of Jews has suffered more severely for a longer period of time than these Sephardic Anusim Jews, as we shall see in Chapter two which surveys this history.

Despite their sufferings, Moses foretold that God would "fetch" and bring them into the land of their forefathers. And he also declared that God plans to do well to them and to multiply them "above their fathers." The Jews I'm referring, specifically the descendants of Inquisition survivors of Spain, Portugal and Mexico have been multiplying in every conceivable way.

Prophetic Precedence

The Prophet Jeremiah affirms the attitude in which God intends to return the Jewish people from the farthest corners of the world. He said,

> *Yea, I will rejoice over them to do them good, and I will plant them in this land in truth with My whole heart and with My whole soul.*[6]

Jeremiah asserts that God will take good pleasure in (re)planting His children back in the land of their forefathers. He also says that God will do this transplanting "with all my heart and soul." There is no other Scripture that declares this more impassionedly.

The Prophet Isaiah emphasizes that God is going to "bring all your brothers, from all the nations, to my holy mountain in Jerusalem."[7] And one of the nations cited is "Tarshish"[8] which many scholars declare is a southern region of ancient Spain; in a location also known as "Tartesos." It is my persuasion that the location of ancient Spain goes all the way back to King Solomon, when he sent fleets of ships every three years to Tarshish in partnership with the Phoenician King Hiram.[9]

The Prophet Zechariah said:

> Thus saith the LORD of hosts: Behold, I will save My people from the east country, and from the west country; And I will bring them, and they shall dwell in the midst of Jerusalem; and they shall be My people, and I will be their God, in truth and in righteousness.[10]

In his vision, Zechariah saw that God shall reach out not only to the nations in the Eastern Hemisphere but also to those in the Western Hemisphere. I believe this Western Hemisphere includes the land mass known as the "New World" of the Americas.

I believe the most relevant Scripture dealing with the Sephardic Anusim is found in the smallest book of the bible, the Prophet Obadiah as he foretells:

> ...and the captivity of Jerusalem, that is in Sepharad, shall possess the cities of the South (Negev). And saviours shall come up on mount Zion to judge the mount of Esau; and the kingdom shall be the LORD'S.[11]

In Hebrew *Sepharad* is Spain. This ancient prophet is foretelling that the Jews of Sepharad/Spain shall possess the cities of the South which is the Negev Desert in southern Israel.

Talmudic Corroboration

> *The Rabbis teach that he who builds the wall is great, But greater is he who stands in the gap.*

There is a Scripture in the Talmud that speaks directly about the Sephardic Anusim. There are rabbis that choose to interpret it differently as is demonstrated in their attitude towards the Anusim but there is an increasing number that are taking a new outlook at this phenomena. The term I am referring to is *tinnok shenishba beyin hagoim*.[12]

Dr. Rabbi Marc D. Angel of New York City revealed to me a personal concern I have held regarding the Sephardic Anusim whom I represent.[13] The quotation below reflects his personal version of the term, *tinnok shenishba beyin hagoim,* and it reads:

> *This term refers to a (Jewish) baby who was captured and raised among non-Jews. Such a child cannot later be held responsible for not knowing the laws of the Torah, since he/she grew up without even knowing he/she was Jewish. Yet, when such a person later learns he/she is of Jewish parentage, he/she can (should) be considered part of the Jewish people and become subject to the laws of the Torah as he/she learns them.*[14]

The term I have quoted is crucially important to the quest of Sephardic Anusim for obvious reasons. It is more relevant to the Sephardic Anusim now particularly because it is a well established fact that the primary religion of the Land of Israel is Judaism; and the authorities that are in high positions of influence are rabbis and Jewish sages. This Talmudic declaration is vital to the furtherance of our research as well as our advocating in favor of the Sephardic Anusim when it comes to their hope of becoming an Israeli citizen. It is for this reason that I cite certain foundational issues which confirms the need for us to have some working knowledge of what the Talmud has to say regarding issues such as those affecting Sephardic Anusim.

In its simplest definition, the Talmud is the record of the discussions that took place across many centuries expounding on the Oral Law of Judaism. These discussions took place in the highest Torah academies of the Land of Israel as well as Babylonia long ago. Throughout Jewish history, the Jewish people in all of their lands of dispersion, basically lived a Talmudic way of life, differing little from the way of the lives of their ancestors in Babylonia during the period of the compilation and editing of the Talmud.[15] Nonetheless, Sephardic Anusim began to lose touch with Talmudic teachings during the obscure ages of Inquisitions in Iberia which followed into the New World.

Chapter Two – Historical Evidences

Origins and Development of Hispanic Jewry
How & When Jews Became Spanish

The fact that Jews got all the way from Israel down the Mediterranean to Spain is a most amazing story. King David and Solomon, his son, had no idea that one day the Jews they sent on explorations to Tarshish,[16] (ancient Spain) would become the fathers of today's Sephardic Anusim. Centuries later, they would become the Maimonides, the Abravanels, Cristobal Colons, the Carvajals, Oñate and the de Vargas of recent centuries as we now see them in our history books.

This story is so full of mystery that it began with Solomon's fleets and ends with fleeing. It moves from wealth, aristocracy and nobility to the confiscation of all their goods and assets in a land their own fathers founded together with their Phoenician cousins. However, the story doesn't begin this way—it actually begins with continuous successes leading to amazing wealth which eventually led to the Golden Age. It began with King David's intimate relationship with the Phoenician Emperor, King Hiram which is in modern day Lebanon.

History, including the Bible, reveals that the Phoenicians were expert ship builders and navigators.[17] It was in those days that King Solomon and King Hiram would send fleets of ships every three years to explore and bring back gold, silver, exotic animals and fruits from different areas of ancient Spain.

These were the initial beginnings when social systems were established all the way from the ports of Israel and Lebanon down to Spain—with North Africa and Europe on either side of the ocean. Some believe that Solomon used some of the gold to adorn the amazing First Temple in the heart of Jerusalem.

After Solomon died, the kingdom of Israel got divided in two with one capital in the north and the other in the south. The northern Kingdom of Israel became very decadent but many Jews of the ten northern tribes chose to unite with the Southern Kingdom of Judah. There is no question that according to the Tanakh or the Old Testament, that Israelites from the north chose to dwell alongside their southern Judean brothers.

It is believed that about 50 years before the Empire of Babylon descended on Jerusalem to destroy and take Jewish captives into exile, many of the Levites, priests and followers fled to Spain.[18] They took with them not only their Hebrew language and Mosaic faith but also certain objects from the Temple; after all, many were Levites and Cohanim.[19] One would ask, but why flee to Spain? They fled to Spain because there was a community of Jews prospering there since the days of Solomon so eventually they became known as the Sephardim not just 'the Jews of Spain.'

I have no doubt that similar flights took place from Israel to Spain during the Syrian oppression under Antiochus IV in 169 BCE. However, the most massive Diaspora of that era took place in 70 CE when the Roman Empire devastated Jerusalem and the "Second Temple," murdered tens of thousands and took over a million Jews to various slave communities throughout Europe. Many Spanish historians believe it was at this time that Jews founded Spain; but now we know this came around 1000 years earlier.

For the following 600 to 700 years after this, Jews prospered and lived peacefully in Spain until major outbreaks of anti-Semitism began to take place all across Spain. From here on out, Jews were constantly targeted for violent persecution. Despite the fact that Sephardim took the lead in ushering in the Golden Age between 1000 and 1400 CE—with displays of great wealth and prosperity, yet on the other hand massacres, riots and all types of violence fell upon the Jewish community of Spain. Year after year, violent crimes were perpetrated against Sephardic Jews until they were forcefully thrown out of their homeland of Sepharad.

Secrets that developed during the Inquisition

The essence of being a Jew in hiding reached its height during these tumultuous times of the Inquisition.[20] Sephardic Jews became the scape goats for anything that went wrong all across Spain.[21] The primary reason for hiding their identity was for shear survival. Sephardic Jews became the primary object of the "Curse of the Inquisition" as they were perpetually victimized. Not being a long-line Catholic was synonymous with being accursed and therefore lumped together with heretics and witches.

They became the target for religious reasons but predominantly because of greed—in other words, Jews had what others wanted and they managed to take it from them by force. Rather than to live a life in constant terror and in hiding, many chose not to convert to Roman Catholicism and fled to countries in Western and Central Europe as well as North Africa and parts of Asia.

As early as 1391,[22] there was a massive Diaspora out of Spain and many fled to countries east of the Great Atlantic. Those that chose to remain in Spain were forced to convert yet they continued to be Jewish at heart. The covert theme of their lives can be characterized by the old saying: "A Catholic by day and a Jew by night."

Consequently, the Inquisition forced remaining Jews to go underground as they perfected their skills as Crypto or hidden Jews. By the time they were expelled in 1492, most of them had adopted a

Crypto Jewish life style.[23] Today many of them prefer to be known as Sephardic Anusim or Benei Anusim meaning 'the people of Anusim.' These are those that were forced or coerced to convert while spiritually and secretly they remained Jewish at heart.

Of recent, we have begun to discover stories of clever methods that were used in order to throw off members of the Catholic legion of Inquisitors and their compatriots. In simple terms, Crypto Jews or Anusim lived a dual life known as, "Cultural Catholics." In other words, they became *Catolicos solamente de nombre,* meaning "Catholics merely by name," with a Jewish heart.

Conflict between Conversos and non-Conversos

The saddest thing that could've taken place, did in fact take place. The Jewish community that had flourished for many centuries began to slowly become fragmented and divided. This wasn't a matter of a few months or years but a crescendo that developed across many centuries. The cause for this was the issue of conversion, whether their conversion was sincere or insincere, it didn't matter.[24]

The Inquisitors and their Catholic cohorts began to label "converted" Jews by calling them *Marranos* [25] [26] (swine, hogs, pigs) and forced them to eat pork in public. Sadly, some of their own Jewish family that did not convert picked up on this labeling, but not to the same proportion as the Catholic community and its Inquisitors. It is impossible to assess how many fell on one side of this 'conversion camp' or the other. However, it is my personal opinion that possibly the majority of those that thought they could ride out the Inquisition storm underwent conversion in order to save their lives and their families. However, there is no question that some of the Sephardim that converted to Catholicism were sincere. This created yet another reason for tension among all Sephardic Jews, regardless of their public or private faith.

They really believed the day would come when the social climate would change, the Inquisition would go away and they could return to a normal life with their faith and Sephardic way of doing things. Those that had the means and fled into North Africa where favor was afforded them at that time eventually discovered the anti-Semitic spirit among their Arab Islamic cousins. Therefore, some of them became Crypto Jews of a different kind; instead of having Catholicism to contend with they now had Islam to endure.

Sad to say, but some Sephardic families that never converted to Catholicism (or were successful in hiding the secret of their ancestors' conversion) have continued to stigmatize Anusim even to this day. A major way in which we evidence this is by the cynical and suspicious eye against Crypto Jews. This is despite the fact that many Crypto Jews are earnest learners that yearn to reconnect with their extended Jewish family. Some of them have discovered they're not welcomed in their synagogues or their social events. The primary reason is because of their Christian theologies and often because of certain dogmatism which influences them to make statements that are questionable and at times offensive to Jews in general.

However, in recent years, I have personally experienced a significant change towards the good in this age old trend. This is a present day phenomenon to see that this five hundred year old secret is beginning to dismantle as our people are learning how to relate to their history as well as to their Jewish family.

The Inquisition in Mexico and New Mexico

The first waves of Sephardic Anusim that fled the fires of the Spanish and the Portuguese Inquisition arrived in the New World thinking, hoping they had come far away enough to put this hellishness behind them forever.[27]

It was only about three decades after Columbus' arrival that all hell broke loose in their new home in *La Nueva Espana* (New Spain) which is Mexico. By 1524, the Spanish Crown had sent a dozen Franciscan clergy to replicate the Spanish Inquisition in downtown Mexico City.[28] I've seen material evidences of this holocaust in the land where our grandparents and great grand parents lived just south of the border.

This was because letters were sent to the Spanish Crown that *La Gente Prohibida* (the "prohibited people") had managed to cross the Atlantic into Mexico. The question is, who were these prohibited people, and what were they prohibited from? When Sephardim were expelled from Spain they were strictly prohibited from crossing the Atlantic Ocean. They could flee to any other country or continent they wished but not across the Atlantic.

Three years after the Franciscans arrived, a dozen Dominican clergy were sent in 1527 in order to fuel the fires of the Inquisition.[29] Their mission was to step up methods to identify and to harshly deal with the Marrano Anusim that had already begun to prosper and to multiply. We must not forget that these Dominicans were after the order of Tomas de Torquemada, the Inquisitor General during King Ferdinand and Queen Isabella. He was an expert in torture and wrote the manual of procedures and interrogation which encompassed the explicit use of torture, both physical and psychological.

In 1571, approximately fifty years after the Dominicans arrived, the High Tribunal of the Inquisition was established in Mexico City. It was around this time that members of Don Luis de Carvajal's land grant known as *El Nuevo Reino del Leon* began to cross the Rio Grande into South Texas.[30] This land grant included my native city of San Antonio, Texas, parts of Dallas, all the way to El Paso, Texas and beyond. This land grant measured around 320,000 square miles (between northern Mexico and parts of the Southwest of the USA.[31]

Not long after this, despite being the Viceroy directly under Spanish King Philip II, don Luis died in a secret Inquisition prison in Mexico City on February 15, 1591. His sister, three daughters and a son were burned alive at the stake in Mexico City just five years later on December 8, 1596 – all because they were Jews.[32]

Just about two years after Don Luis' family was burned alive at the stake, Don Juan de Oñate, a Sephardic Conquistador, succeeded in leading his group of Sephardic Anusim across the Rio Grande through El Paso, Texas and into New Mexico in 1598.[33][34] Had it not been for him the remnant of Sephardic Anusim may have been decimated. Oñate became the first Governor and Captain-General of New Mexico at this time. Besides the members of his own group I earnestly believe he brought with him some of the remnants of Don Luis' group.

The main hub of their initial establishment was in Santa Fe, New Mexico. Nonetheless, they settled throughout all of New Mexico and Southern Colorado, especially Northern New Mexico. Oñate established his capital near Ohkay Owingeh Pueblo which is formerly known as San Juan Pueblo, about 25 miles north of Santa Fe.

Meanwhile, Don Pedro de Peralta became New Mexico's third governor. He formally founded Santa Fe and gave it its full name, *La Villa Real de la Santa Fe de San Francisco de Assisi*, or the "Royal City of the Holy Faith of Saint Francis of Assisi." Santa Fe was formally founded in 1608 and made the capital in 1610, making it the oldest capital city in the United States of America. Between the years 1680-1692, Native Pueblo people drove the Sephardim out of New Mexico. Don Diego de Vargas re-conquered it in 1692.[35]

Santa Fe remained Spain's provincial seat until the outbreak of the Mexican War of Independence in 1810. In 1824 the city's status as the capital of the Mexican territory of Santa Fé de Nuevo México was formalized in the 1824 Constitution of the United States.

The story of Santa Fe paralells the story of Monterrey, Mexico which became the capital of the State of Nuevo Leon in Mexico; but much earlier than Santa Fe. We're barely finding out that there are many other cities, towns and regions that were first pioneered by Sephardic Anusim throughout our nation's Southwest. But I believe it is the privilege of New Mexican Anusim to serve as a guiding light to all those that are barely awakening from a 500 year "corporate state of amnesia." After all, they have kept the torch of their Sephardic presence aflame since the days when their forefather began to go underground as Crypto-Jews.

Customs and other Evidences of Sephardic Anusim

There are many evidences that point directly to the existence of Sephardic roots among Hispanic/Latinos throughout the Southwest, particularly Texas and New Mexico. Some of these include: onomastics which deals with *appellidos* or surnames; genealogies, material evidences such as gravestones; oral histories; the recent frontier of DNA; as well as customs, practices, traditions and Ladino terms. I would like to simply refer to a few of these evidences.[36]

Most of the prevalent evidences in the arena of Sephardic customs, practices, traditions and terms were performed in hiding. The following is a sampling of a few of the experiences I personally experienced during my growing up days and I continue to see how they affect my life.

Celebrating Shabbat (Sabbath), feasts and holy gatherings

A most common practice was that many lit candles on the eve of the Sabbath (Shabbat). They didn't always have white candles so they used colorful ones to adorn the room. Since they were portraying to be Catholics, they often had candles lit to the saints so as to throw off any potential spy. Some had a hidden place in the house where the family would gather together to pray, to celebrate the holy feasts and to remember the lives of their Sephardic ancestry.

Using Sephardic methods for cooking and butchering

Many used a kosher method of butchering animals by draining and burying the blood and carefully trimming sinews from the animal. Many would personally fatten a lamb and butcher it for Passover; this was referred to as *el cordero Pascual,* meaning "the Passover lamb." While women made *la masa* (the dough) for tortillas, a tiny lump of dough was cast into the open fire. In fact, flower tortillas became the matzo of Sephardic Anusim of Northern Mexico and the Southwest while the corn tortilla was for those in southern Mexico.

Hiding Jewish relics and other paraphernalia

Some hid mezuzahs behind picture frames near the thresholds inside their homes. Some hid menorahs in secret places such as basements and attics.

Practicing peculiar methods during the death and dying process

Upon the death of a family member, the mirrors were covered; and their place in the dinning table was left vacant for weeks or months after their death. In some instances, the meal that corresponded to the deceased was given to a beggar or homeless individual. It was a Sephardic tradition for men to carve their own gravestone and allow no one to see it until the day they died; at which time the family discovered Jewish letters or symbols on it. Sephardic artists would often place small Hebrew letters on Catholic buildings and paintings

Communicating in an archaic Ladino dialect

Even though many of our fathers and forefathers attempted to purge their lives of such customs and traditions, their language was a 'dead-giveaway' to those that knew any better. Language is so integral to the conscious and unconscious mind; we find many vestiges of the Ladino expression which is the language of Sephardic Jews.

Here are a few examples of the Ladino expressed in the Southwest of the USA and throughout certain regions of Latin America such as northern Mexico.

Many of my generation and those before me have been criticized for using what is called "dirty Spanish," meaning improper Spanish.[37] The point of the matter was that it wasn't intended to be proper Spanish but the dialect of Sephardim which is Ladino. Grant it, Ladino took on various words, terms and intonations depending on the region where they lived, nonetheless, the root of it was still Ladino. The fact is that most of these archaic terms existed way before "proper Spanish" was defined as such. After all, it wasn't until 1726 when the Royal Academy of Language published its first official dictionary.[38] In other words, the

Ladino terms our people used came way before this Royal Dictionary as well as before the Academies in Latin America.

It's a wonder how so many of these old archaic terms have prevailed throughout these centuries, here's a brief example of terms:

- *Mercar* instead of comprar
- *Ueno* or *weno* instead of bueno which means "good"
- *Semos* instead of somos which means "we are"
- *Ansina* instead of asi which means "like this" or "like that"
- *Chante* instead of hogar meaning home
- *Antiuo* instead of antiguo meaning old or ancient
- *Abujero* instead of agujero meaning a "hole"
- *Desden antes* instead of desde antes meaning "since before"
- *Se caldio* instead of se enojo meaning "he/she got very upset"
- *Que sura* meaning "how terrible" or "how disgusting"
- *Se relajo* meaning he chickened out. In proper Spanish it means to relax; but in times of the Inquisition it described a person that was burnt at the stake – this term is called *relajación.*
- A few other modern colloquialisms are: *troque* for truck, *cuera* for young woman, *canton* for home, *grifo* for irate but it can also mean a drug addict.

As I close this historical section I am vividly aware of the amount of work that is yet before us in terms of reconstructing the mosaic of Sephardic Anusim's past in conjunction with its promising future. What is most amazing to me is not so much the fact that we still have historical records after so many centuries filled with attempted annihilations and holocausts. But the most incredible thing is that we still have any descendants of the victims of so many holocausts and Inquisitions that persisted across hundreds of years and thousands of miles. It stands to reason that there must, therefore, still be a cause, a purpose and an unfilled destiny that is yet to be fulfilled.

Chapter Three – Material Evidences

Material evidences are those objects that convey a message which help us understand what was on the minds of the people of that time. Many of these objects are inscribed with letters, signs, words or symbols which tell a story. In the case of Sephardic Anusim, these messages are sometimes found in a foreign language such as Hebrew, Phoenician or Paleo-Hebrew as well as archaic Spanish.

The evidences recorded here serve to confirm the historical record and tell a story of a people which even DNA can not provide. They range from hidden objects recently discovered, gravestones, symbols on ancient paintings as well as Hebrew signs on buildings and other physical locations including boulders on mountains and hills.

The following material evidences support the presence of Jewish roots among Sephardic Latinos in the USA as well as Mexico. I have only included a few evidences that corroborate the record in this book. There are untold hundreds and perhaps thousands of other evidences throughout our hemisphere. Some of them are secretly tucked away in homes; others are on display in libraries, museums and institutions of higher learning. Yet others lay dormant in obscure places yet to be unearthed and interpreted.

The following section demonstrates thirteen material objects which prove the presence of Hebrew roots among Sephardic Latinos of the Southwest in the USA. They range from gravestones to hidden mezuzahs, from paintings held in public places to epigraphy engraved on rock and boulders, from symbols in religious institutions to a few of the actual instruments that were used to torture Jews in various Inquisitions including Mexico.

The Hidden Mezuzah

One of my earliest discoveries in the realm of material evidences came as a surprise shared with me by special friend in New Mexico.[39] He and other members of his family had some oral histories that related to being of an old Crypto-Sephardic lineage. This is a reconstruction of his story as told to me in 2004.

One day, he visited an abandoned ancestral home in southern New Mexico. The house was in disrepair without hope of rebuilding. As he walked through the interior of the home where his grandmother (or great grandmother) once lived, reminiscing on the many wonderful memories he noticed a plank of wood on the threshold going from one room to another. Having a creative mind, he felt he should yank it off in order to do something artistic with it. When he succeeded in doing so, he noticed a cubby hole behind the plank he had just removed.

Inside this hole was a tiny gold box. The lid had mother of pearl inlaid and in the center was a beautiful gold Star of David. I felt honored to handle it myself. When I cautiously opened this tiny box, there was a most amazing Mezuzah inside of it. Mezuzahs contain Hebrew Scriptures of the Torah within it. Many Jewish families place a Mezuzah on the thresholds of most doors entering and exiting the house and almost every room in the home.

The Jewish tradition is that as a person enters a room, they first touch the Mezuzah and often kiss their hand before and/or after having touched it. This is to demonstrate utter respect for the contents of the Torah within it.

One day, Ruben visited his uncle, one of the oldest surviving members of the family. He inquired of him in these approximate words, *Tio, que tenia buelita alli sobre tal y tal puerta en su casa?* ("Uncle, what did grandmother have over such and such a door in her home?") The uncle's response was more or less, "*Ooo, alli tenia un retrato de San Martin de Porras...y cada vez que pasaba por alli lo bezaba* (Ohhh, she used to have a painting of the Saint Martin of Porras...and every time she passed by it she'd kiss it.")

It is quite obvious that the dear grandmother was not kissing a Catholic saint as much as she was kissing what was hidden behind that saint which was the small gold Mezuzah hid in the little gold box with a Star of David. Below is a photo I took of this intriguing box and its contents. Pardon the photo–it was the best I could do under the circumstances.

Small box with gold Star of David (left)
and Mezuzah inside box (right)

The Different Gravestone

After seeing Ruben's amazing Mezuzah, we visited an old cemetery of a humble Catholic mission in Southern New Mexico.[40] This *campo santo* (holy ground) was overgrown with weeds and thorns that would stick to our clothing at a simplest brush. Each of the three of us took different routes in our search for symbols that could possibly be Hebraic in nature. As hidden as it was, it stood out from all the rest because of its construction design and the Spanish as well as Hebrew letters inscribed on it.

None of us knew enough Hebrew to know what the Hebrew letters meant. I was able to decipher the Spanish words but not the Hebrew ones. My concern was why would this gravestone have the sign of a cross if, in fact, the person buried beneath this gravestone was Jewish? Suddenly, I remembered that many Crypto-Jews who were once called *Marranos* would do everything conceivable to mislead the Catholic authorities and their spies who would identify individuals or families practicing anything Jewish. So many Sephardic Crypto Jews would place a visible cross so as to inform all Catholics that they, too, were Catholic; even though they were only *Catolicos meramente de nombre,* (Catholics only by name). I refer to this phenomenon as "Cultural Catholics." By revealing Catholic signs and symbols, they avoided persecution and in olden days they would also avoid repercussions from the Roman Catholic Inquisition, its inquisitors and conspirators.

One day, while lecturing in the Ben Gurion Heritage Institute in the heart of the Negev Desert of Israel, I shared this story and showed my audience the photo I had taken of this peculiar gravestone. I admitted that I could interpret the Spanish words but not the Hebrew ones, if in fact they were Hebrew. At that moment, a Jewish scholar raised her hand and said, "Oh, but I know Hebrew very well." At the exact moment I experienced relief and grief because I didn't know if my theory would be disproved and I'd wind up embarrassed for my ignorant assumptions.

This scholarly Israeli came up from her seat and stood in front of the screen and said, "Ah ha, it's Hebrew okay. These are the letters portraying the first five of the Ten Commandments." Oh, the relief I felt of such an incredible finding I was a part of. A few years later, I discovered that this very gravestone is on the cover of my colleague and friend's latest book, "To the ends of the earth," by Dr. Stanley Hordes, former historian for the State of New Mexico.[41]

Here is the photo I took on that special day in that old Catholic *campo santo*.

Gravestone with Hebrew & Spanish inscriptions

Hebrew letters on gravestone in Santa Fe

One winter season in 2007, we ventured on an investigative and lecture tour through New Mexico. Despite blizzards and record breaking snow in northern New Mexico, Helen and I managed to scout another cemetery in Santa Fe, New Mexico, north of down town.[42] We trudged through knee high snow searching for hints of Sephardic connotations among the gravestones there. I had already read about Sephardic Crypto

Jews obscuring certain Jewish symbolisms such as the use of the six pedal flowers to symbolize the Star of David. In fact, the more we searched through cemeteries across New Mexico, we discovered a good number of these gravestones with six point flowers. However, in our inquisitive search we bumped into a peculiar gravestone with actual Hebrew inscriptions.

We were able to confirm that the gravestone illustrated below is, in fact, the Hebrew letters portraying the name of God which are the letters YHVH.[43] Whoever requested this gravestone had the courage to not only inscribe these eternal letters portraying God's Name but to also place the photo of the dearly deceased. Below is the photo of this gravestone. Note the Hebrew letters of the Name of God beneath the photo.

Gravestone of Trinidad V. Gonzalez

Gravestone with Menorah and Star of David in Coyote, New Mexico

After sharing our story with Isabella, heiress of Isaac Morfin, she told us of the peculiar gravestone her uncle had chiseled and not to be seen until the day he died. They placed his self constructed stone at the head of his grave in a private cemetery on the mountainous back woods between Coyote and Gallina, New Mexico. When we explained what the inscriptions meant to Isabella, she blurted out, "I never knew my uncle was a Crypto-Jew." I can earnestly say that Isaac Morfin fit the "classic" model of what it means to be a Sephardic Jew in hiding.

The gravestone speaks for itself as you will notice a Jewish Menorah inside the Star of David on the upper right hand side of the gravestone. Signs and symbols such as these are found in old cemeteries throughout the State of New Mexico.

Isaac Morfin's gravestone

Stars of David in Old Catholic Church

Smack in the middle of the Old Town Albuquerque Plaza stands San Felipe de Neri Catholic Church.[44] See illustration below.

Photo of structure of old San Felipe Church

As I entered the sanctuary and walked towards the altar, my eyes got glued on two Jewish symbols. On both sides of its simple yet ornate altar, there they were, two large Stars of David. I later discovered through oral histories that this church was funded by a wealthy Jew who was rescued by a Catholic bishop and his military entourage as the Jewish family was under an attack by Indian rebels. The oral history says that the Jewish man was so grateful that he loan the money for this church to be built; however, he later changed his mind and donated the money with the condition that these Stars of David be placed where they are today. Notice the Stars of David at both ends of the arch of the altar. (Pardon my photos.)

Inside San Felipe Church with Stars of David over altar

Hebrew letters at main entrance of Catholic Cathedral

We had seen the Stars of David in the old Albuquerque Church but we knew nothing about a new discovery we made without expecting it. Of all places, this was in the center of the Old Plaza of Santa Fe, New Mexico.

As we scaled the steps to the main entrance of the St. Francis of Assisi Catholic Cathedral, keeping our eyes wide open for any hint of Jewish symbolism, lo and behold, as we stared up at the arched entrance, there it was, plain as day.[45] The same Hebrew letters portraying the Name of God were sculptured on the very top of the entrance archway, YHVH, but in Hebrew. The three of us on this scouting mission were at awe with something as incredible as the Hebrew Name of God on the central entrance of a Roman Catholic Cathedral.

Approximately 76 years after San Felipe de Neri Catholic Church was built in Old Albuquerque, Archbishop Lamy commissioned the construction of St. Francis of Assisi Catholic Cathedral in 1869.

Structure of St. Francis Catholic Cathedral

Arch with Hebrew letters atop St. Francis Catholic Cathedral

Hebrew letters on old Painting of the Virgin Mary

After some years in my search for evidences, I began to wonder if there might be any material evidences in my hometown of San Antonio as well as in south-central Texas. After all, Sephardic Crypto Jews entered Texas before entering any other state including New Mexico. For instance, historian/archivist Richard Santos specifically declares that as early as 1576-77 they were in "What would later be called South Central Texas."[46] The reason for stating, "what would be later called South Central Texas" is because that part of the region was within the "kingdoms of Spain"; therefore, it was in what is today known as Mexico. The 1848 U.S.-Mexican Treaty of Guadalupe Hidalgo delivered Texas into America's hands. Initially, Texas belonged to Mexico and was formerly part of a Spanish kingdom known as *El Nuevo Reino del Leon* (The New Kingdom of the Lion).

San Antonio has always been a very Catholic city with the existence of many Catholic churches, old cathedrals and Spanish Missions. Perhaps, one reason for my not identifying as many evidences in Texas is because we have spent much time on the road and much more time studying the phenomenal awakening and evidences of Sephardic Crypto-Jews in New Mexico than any other place including Texas.

One day, Terry, a family friend visited some of the Catholic Spanish Missions in San Antonio. One of the five Spanish Missions in San Antonio is the oldest one, San Antonio de Valero, commonly known as The Alamo, built in 1718. The fourth oldest Mission in San Antonio is Mission *Concepcion* (Conception). It was founded by Franciscan friars in East Texas in 1716 and moved to San Antonio in 1731.[47]

As Terry carefully observed the architectural design of the Mission along with its remnants and paintings, she discovered a most peculiar sign atop an old painting of the Virgin Mary. Never had I seen such an inscription on a Catholic painting. As the Virgin stands with open arms, surrounded by twelve stars around her head, there appears the Hebrew letters of the Name of God, YHVH. These are the exact letters we found on top of the archway entrance of St. Francis of Assisi

Catholic Cathedral in Santa Fe, New Mexico as well as the gravestone in the Santa Fe cemetery. It is worth noting that these same letters appear constantly in the Torah. (It is noteworthy to state that I am not attempting to legitimize any Catholic artwork because of the presence of Hebraic implications but am merely pointing out a fact.)

Virgin Mary Painting

Mystery of Hidden Mountain–Epigraphy

I had heard reports that there existed a large stone boulder with the inscription of the Ten Commandments in ancient Paleo-Hebrew on Hidden Mountain near Los Lunas, New Mexico. The original name stated in archives has this mountain as *Serro de los Escondidos*, meaning "Mountain of the hidden ones."[48] It is believed by some of the local Crypto Jews that went underground during their flight from the Mexican and later the New Mexican Inquisition that a group of Sephardic Crypto Jews dwelled there. Some believe this was a holy location where Cohanim Jews of the ancient High Priestly line of Aaron hid and preserved their Sephardic faith, customs and traditions. Along with this came the preservation of Hebrew's most ancient language known as Phoenician-Hebrew or Paleo-Hebrew.

As stated in the segment on "Historical Evidences," King David and King Solomon had a very special partnership with King Hiram of the Phoenician Empire. Some have speculated that the epigraphy[49] on this boulder dates back to those times. Others have theorized that many of the Cohanim fled Jerusalem years before the Babylonian Exile of 586 BCE. Since Jews had already settled in Spain during King Solomon's era, these Cohanim brought with them many vestiges of their faith as well as their ancient Hebrew script including Paleo-Hebrew. Since we continue to have evidences of the Cohanim DNA haplogroups, especially in New Mexico, it is possible that some of their Cohanim ancestors carefully chiseled the Decalogue on the boulder on Hidden Mountain.

The hike up this Hidden Mountain is quite rigorous, dusty and dry. Unless you have directions, chances are you will never find it. During my first hike up this mountain, we made a few stops to catch our breath and sip on fresh water before continuing on. At one point, I was panting so hard that when we finally reached this holy location, I had not noticed that this incredible boulder with the Ten Commandments was standing right by my side. I could hardly believe my eyes; I didn't know what to think or even how to act. I was utterly stunned. Since that initial discovery, I have returned with others and when they get there, they too are astonished by this amazing masterpiece of Paleo-Hebraic inscription of the Ten Commandments.

There are other amazing inscriptions in Paleo-Hebrew on boulders higher up the mountain as well as Native Indian hand paintings (petroglyphs) on a ragged cliff of this lonely mountain. However, in recent years some ignorant persons have scaled up the mountain and have begun to chisel away at the Decalogue thus destroying parts of it. But when I first saw it, it was in tact and complete as can be seen in the photo below.

Decalogue Stone & Dell Sanchez on Hidden Mountain

Shift in focus of Material Evidences

I shall now shift from material evidences which portray positive discoveries to those that imposed grave suffering upon the Sephardic Anusim. I'm referring to an investigative journey Helen and I took in 2002 to key spots in Old Mexico. One of our primary objectives was to explore possible locations and methods used against Sephardic Anusim by the Mexican Inquisition. As stated in the "Historical Evidences" section above, the Mexican Inquisition was birthed in 1525 and lasted around 300 years. It continues to amaze me how very few people know about this slow holocaust that brought such prolonged dismay to its victims. These Jewish victims had just fled the Inquisitions in Spain and Portugal only to discover that its diabolical ghosts followed them all the way across the Great Atlantic.

We discovered an array of evidences in the cities of Monterrey, the Port of Tampico and the Port of Vera Cruz.[50] The city I wish to focus on was the central hub of the Inquisition in Mexico City. Our main findings took us to the *Sector Colonial* (Colonial Section) in the heart of Mexico City where most of the ancient buildings and evidences continue to stand erect after 500 years. This mega city is magnificent in artwork, architectural design, literary prodigies as well as pre and post Columbian history. The cultural climate is rich in all aspects including its international flavor.

What we discovered is far more than what is revealed in the pages of this book. Since our goal was to identify the various types of evidences of the Mexican Inquisition and how it targeted the *Marranos* or *Conversos,* I shall therefore focus on the atrocious instruments that were used to perpetrate on these people.

Mexican Inquisition Burning at the Stake Location

Our primary goal was to find any form of evidences that were used to torture Sephardic Anusim victims. The first place we wished to visit was *El Palacio de la Inquisicion*–the Palace of the Inquisition. Every inquisition in the Old as well as the New World had a palace. We had a deep sense we would find something peculiar in or near the Inquisition's Palace. We knew it would not be easy because its name had been changed but we knew it was somewhere in the large Colonial Sector of the sprawling downtown area of Mexico City.

Our instinct was to head straight to the heart of *El Sector Colonial* to find that illusive "Palace" where so many atrocities were decreed and took place in its subterranean area. We knew that we would find it but it would not be an easy task because many of the local citizens were unfamiliar with the existence of the Mexican Inquisition.

In our search, we discovered what turned out to be a Catholic convent with locked steel gates held together by two large rock pillars. As I stood peering through the gates trying to get a decent photograph, my wife stood a few feet behind me looking at the bigger picture of this amazing structure. Suddenly I heard her say something that sounded like an unexpected discovery when she said, "Come see what it says here." There on the two stone pillars were signs in colonial Spanish.

The sign on one of the pillars declared the name of the building which we were starring at. The name was San Diego Convent written in Colonial Spanish (as can be seen in the following illustration).[51] So I figured, "Okay, now we know the name of this ancient convent but what happened there?"

To my utter amazement, the other pillar had a sign describing what took place in front of this convent throughout a 175 year period from 1596 to 1771. What took place here began 240 years before the Battle of Alamo and lasted 151 years after the historical landing at Plymouth Rock in 1670.

The sign on this pillar described the diabolical reality of what these Sephardic Crypto Jews suffered in front of this "holy place." The sign on this pillar reads:

> *Frente a este lugar estuvo el quemadero de la Inquisición de 1596 a 1771.*

In English it reads, "In front of this place was the burning at the stake of the Inquisition from 1596 to 1771."

In other words, this was the exact and perhaps primary location of the burnings at the stake known in Spanish as *las hogueras*. In many instances these burnings were as bad as the ovens of Poland's Death Camps. However, in this case they lasted hundreds of years and were performed in public while the majority of victims were still alive. These burnings were performed only after extensive psychological and physical torture in locations known as *La Casa Santa* or "The Holy House." This process is known as *Purificacion de sangre* which, in English means, "Purification of the blood." This meant that after the victim was burned at the stake, their ashes would be cast into a running river or stream so as to erase all memory of the lives of the victims and the manner in which they "contaminated" their communities and society.

The illustration immediately below is that of the actual convent. The next one is the pillar with the name of the convent. The third one shows the actual inscription of the existence of the burnings at the stake.

Photo of actual structure

Combento Sn Diego

Out From Hiding

Photo of pillar and description of Inquisition

Evidences of Torture used on Sephardic Anusim

The next segment of illustrations will reveal only a few of the 82 different torture instruments that were used on Sephardic Anusim.[52] Torture was used in order to force them to convert from Judaism to Roman Catholicism. After their coerced conversion they were forced to eat the unkosher meat of pork and labeled *Marranos* (pigs) for the rest of their lives. The spying mechanisms and informants that were used by Inquisitors and friends of the Inquisition ran rampant throughout the regions of the Inquisition's domain. Many Jews were raped, kidnapped or suddenly disappeared.

It must be noted that the majority of victims that fell to the Mexican Inquisition were Sephardic Jews. They were lumped together with witches and heretics according to the Inquisitors' assessments.

When Sephardic Jews were expelled from Portugal in 1497, all children under the age of fourteen were forced to remain in Portugal and were then placed in Catholic wards. All others were forced to leave the country once and for all.[53] These children and their descendants were raised believing they were Gentiles and living a Roman Catholic lifestyle. It is noteworthy to declare that many of the children of those that were kidnapped or programmed to believe they were Gentiles are waking up to the true reality of their Sephardic Jewish ancestry and are longing to get reconnected to their Jewish family and community. (This is where the Talmudic principle comes in as found in the first chapter under Talmudic Corroboration; namely, *tinnok shenishba beyin hagoim.*)

Please bear with the photos which I personally took. I was inordinately rushed to capture the photos of each and every torture instrument and to properly document what each instrument looked like and how they were used on its victims.

El Garrote – The Garrote

The garrote, better known in Spanish as *El Garrote* was an instrument where the victim would be strapped standing or sitting down with the victim's back against a post. A band was placed around the neck of the victim and slowly tightened by a large crank in the rear of the post. This instrument was used throughout Iberia as well as in the Americas.

The point of this strangulation was the same as in the case of all other torture tools—to inflict horrific pain without killing the person so that they could later process them through a most humiliating *auto de fe*[54] and then burn them at the stake alive. However, as 'an act of mercy,' if the victim confessed before their death and converted to Roman Catholicism, rather than to burn the victim alive, they would turn the crank until he or she was strangled to death. Afterwards their dead bodies would be burned at the stake in what's called *Las Hogueras*.

On a personal note, during my childhood I clearly recall my father and some of his brothers saying, *Ay que garrotiada lleve hoy,*[55] which means, "Oh, what a garroting I experienced today." In my youthful mind, and not knowing what this *garrote* was all about, I used to think they were using another similar word which is *barrote* with the letter "b" rather than "g." In Spanish the term, *barrote* is a heavy beam of wood, something like a four inch square beam or thicker. So I would deduce they were speaking figuratively–and they were. However, they were not saying *barrote* but *garrote*. In other words, at some point during their day someone had persecuted or afflicted them in such a painful way that they felt figuratively garroted or strangled.

The Garrote

Iron Masks[56]

During Adolph Hitler's madness, he demanded all European Jews to wear a Star of David with the word Jew in the middle of it. This lasted for approximately ten years. Meantime, I had known for some years about the *San Benitos* which Sephardic Jews had to wear throughout a period of around 300 years in Iberia and another three hundred years in Mexico and other Latin American nations where there was an Inquisition. These vestures had to be worn publicly along with a tall dunce hat. However, I had no idea that many were forced to also wear an iron mask or heavy chains and necklaces whenever they went out into the public. The illustration below needs no explanation within the context of the suffering Sephardic Anusim was forced to endure.

Iron Masks

The Iberian Inquisitions (Spain and Portugal) together with those in the New World including Mexico were obsessed with various torture weapons. One of their favorite ones was the wheel. The wheels varied in size, construction and structure. Some were made of wood and others were made of iron. The point of this torture method was similar to the infamous rack (*El Potro*) as well as various uses of ropes.[57] Instruments like these were used not only to induce severe pain but also to dismember human bodies. The illustration of the wheel below explains itself.

Out From Hiding

Wheel with Skeleton

La Pera – **The Pear**[58]

The torture instrument below was among the smallest yet immensely excruciating and extremely humiliating, here's why. The Pear had iron points with symbols of demons or devils on it. On the top it had a crank that was used to crank open *La Pera*. It was placed in the mouth or the most private parts of a man or woman regardless of age and then cranked until it dismembered the bone and tendon structure. The illustration below speaks for itself.

The Pear Torture tool

Overview and conclusion of this section

The purpose of this chapter has not been to assess the psychological outcomes of the Inquisition with its varied torture methods. However, it is appropriate to note that that as a mental health professional, I have observed deeply embedded behaviors that may point to a transgenerational syndrome that has afflicted Sephardic Anusim even when they have no concept of what their forefathers were forced to endure. The good news is that, as this book describes, they are coming out of hiding and reconnecting with their ancestral roots and being healed as they recapture the dignity that was robbed of them along with the destiny of their own lives.

Chapter Four – Scientific Evidences

–DNA–

DNA testing has probably been the greatest breakthrough for Sephardic Anusim because it scientifically proves their ancestors were, in fact, Sephardic, with traces of Ashkenazi roots as well. We have also discovered traces of indigenous (native) people that migrated into the Western Hemisphere from parts of Eurasia and its regions nearby thousands of years ago. DNA test results have shown this to be true mostly among the women of Sephardic Anusim.

There is an element of the unknown in what's called "hard science" that intrigues me. What I mean by this has to do with the depth and complexities hidden within evidences that often lie in the realm of the unseen such as genes, molecules and DNA.

We have evidence that the adversaries of Sephardim have never wanted them to find out who they really are. Some of these adversaries happen to be threatened by the existence of DNA roots among people of a Hispanic or Latino background. They didn't mind them finding out their histories because history is subject to the writer. It has been said that "History is what happened to others–never to ourselves." Those who write history are predominantly the champions of a conflict or war. This is why history can be written and interpreted in various different ways. One example is the case of the Battle of the Alamo. The dominant history has always been the American side of the story, but there is another side to it which is the Mexican side, not only told by Mexicans but also by credible American historians.

On the other hand, Sephardic Anusim's enemies have had no problem with oral histories because they give the impression of simple folklore and legends, not the written record of scholarship. They don't even mind the discovery of onomastics—which speaks of the origins and construction of names. And they did not care much about material evidences such as epigraphy and those found on gravestones because who wants to spend great amounts of time and money, traveling far distances into unfamiliar locations or searching through *pantiones* or cemeteries in search for gravestones. They didn't even care much about documents pointing to genealogical findings because most of Sephardic Anusim's ancient records were destroyed by the perpetrators of the Inquisitions in histories past. But when it came to hard, modern science, specifically modern genetic genealogy such as DNA testing–that is a whole different story.

While there are many ways to write and interpret history there are only two ways to interpret science—the right way and the inaccurate way. The levels of significance in scientific findings are not mere theory. In other words, if the same DNA test is taken by different sources using scientific methods, the results should always come out the same. DNA test results, performed by a reputable laboratory with proven experts are significant to the 99.9% degree of accuracy.

The 1980s ushered in the age of DNA testing, which permitted researchers to perform amazing feats of genealogical identification. With current techniques, it is possible for a single person to be differentiated from all the people that have ever lived throughout history by using DNA even from a single root of hair.

DNA has been assisting genetic genealogists in deciphering clues that have been left behind by ancestors even hundreds or thousands of years ago. It has provided a major breakthrough to those that have lost their trail in the process of unearthing documents and connecting with distant relatives that may not have known of each other without the scientific method of DNA.

Alas, I have gone full circle in this quest and end the fourteen year cycle of my investigations with hard scientific facts. Besides this, I am now able to make base line comparisons between Sephardic Jews around the world in conjunction with those, say, of the New Mexico region in comparison to those in Texas. A most gratifying thing for me is to discover that what I have been telling everyone for over fourteen years is finally tested and scientifically proven to be fact, thanks to collaborative DNA testing.

Therefore, the purpose of this chapter is to provide an international model of Sephardic DNA haplogroups[59] through tests gathered from Sephardic Jews around the world. I shall then compare these results to two other DNA projects located in the Southwest of the USA. One project is headquartered in New Mexico and the other in Texas.

The International Sephardim DNA Profile (ISDNAP)

Before assessing DNA test results of the two Southwestern DNA projects and comparing one to the other, I will first give an overview of the International Profile of Sephardic DNA haplogroups.

While I am not a molecular scientist or DNA expert I must say that I do administer a DNA test project in direct conjunction with the "Family Tree DNA" laboratory in Houston, Texas.[60] My role is to put into layman's terms what Sephardic DNA experts are saying in scientific terms which are too complicated for non-scientists to comprehend.

The ISDNAP (International Sephardim DNA Profile) that is demonstrated below was developed by an expert in Sephardic DNA. Until this scientist's findings are published, I am not at freedom to release his name, but I am privy to know of this scientist and have followed his works on the subject. I hope that by the time the book is complete this scientist and his team shall have published their work and I can then reveal their identity and give appropriate credit.

Sephardic males are categorized as belonging to one of nine various DNA haplogroups. These haplogroups generally consist of a capital letter such as "J" or "R" and other letters as can be seen below. Very often the letter comes with a number and lower case letters such as "J1" or "R1b" and so forth.

The ISDNAP has provided the foundation for comparison between it and the two Southwestern DNA projects. Immediately after each haplogroup below is the percentage of Sephardic men that have this same DNA haplogroup. In other words, all Sephardic Jewish men fall into one of nine DNA haplogroups. Percentages are rounded off.

The International Sephardim DNA Profile (ISDNAP)

I = 1% / Q = 2% / K = 3%* / R1a = 4% / E3b1 = 13%

G = 16% / R1b = 13% / J1 = 16% / J2 = 32%

*Haplogroup K has become T

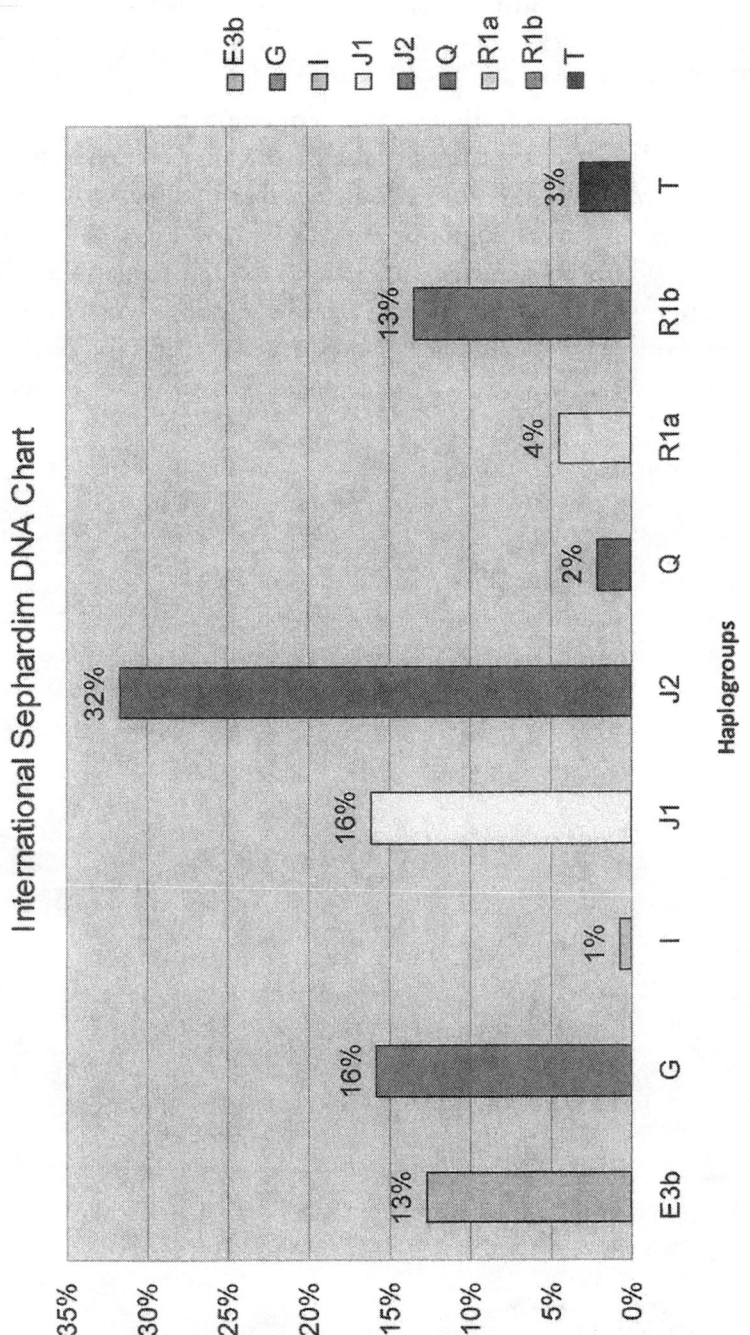

Bar graph #1 of the International Sephardim DNA Chart

Dell F. Sanchez, Ph.D.

The Santa Fe Sephardic DNA Project

The Santa Fe DNA Project is based in Albuquerque, New Mexico and is administered by Catholic Priest William Sanchez. This project consists predominantly of indigenous Latinos of New Mexico. The project is exceptional due to the high number of what I consider to be "classical Jewish haplogroups" which will be explained later in this chapter. This book focuses on 230 out of 237 test results which were gleaned in February 2010 (thanks to father Bill Sanchez for his amazing work in this field). The Santa Fe Project reflects the exact nine haplogroups with their distinct percentages. Percentages are rounded off.

I = 14% / Q = 4% / T = 0% / R1a = 1% / E1b1 = 2%

G = 4% / R1b = 39% / J1 = 20% / J2 = 14%

Out From Hiding

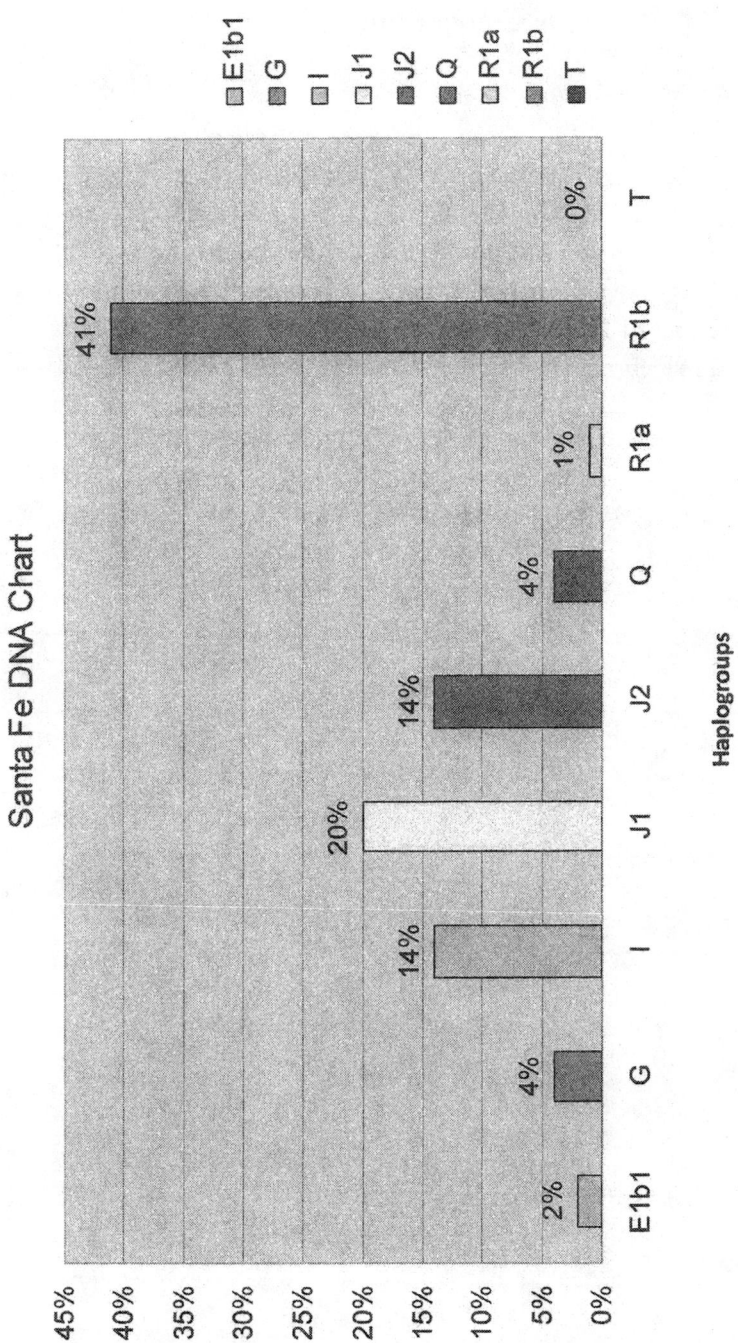

Bar graph #2 of the Santa Fe DNA Chart

Dell F. Sanchez, Ph.D.

The 4Sephardim DNA Project

The next set of DNA results represent the 4Sephardim DNA Project which I administer in conjunction with Family Tree DNA Laboratory in Houston, Texas. The 4Sephardim DNA Project is headquartered in San Antonio, Texas and predominantly represents indigenous Latinos of Texas and a few from other parts of the southern states in the USA. The number of DNA test results in this case was 134 which were also gleaned in February in 2010. Percentages are rounded off.

I = 9% / Q = 7% / T = 1% / R1a = 6% / E1b1 = 13%

G = 6% / R1b = 47% / J1 = 3 % / J2 = 8%

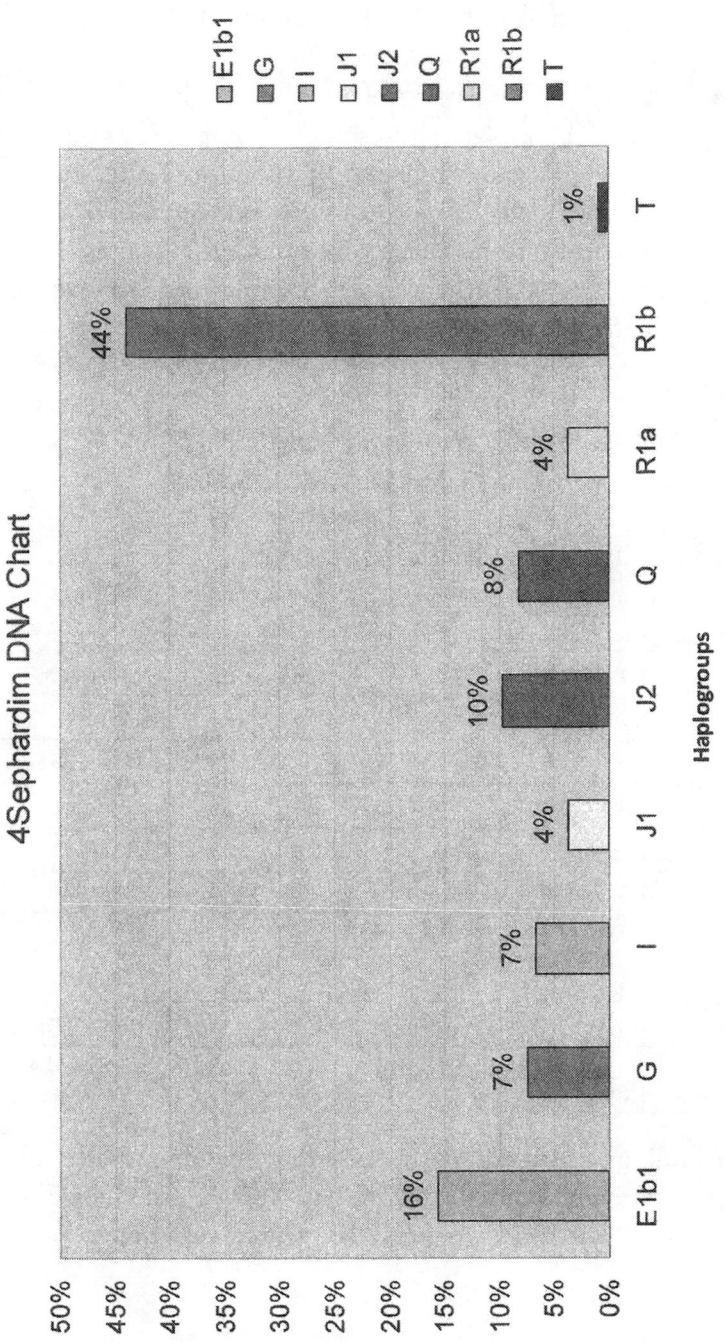

Bar graph #3 of the 4Sephardim DNA Chart

Comparison between Three DNA Projects

In order to adequately compare the numbers between these three projects, I have placed the same columns next to each other. The International Profile is followed by the Santa Fe Project and the 4Sephardim Project. The last two columns on the right consist of the SF (Santa Fe) Project and the 4S (4Sephardim Project). These two columns show the percentage with a plus sign (+) if it is higher than the International Profile or the minus sign (–) if it is lower.

Table 4
Comparison between International Profile,
Santa Fe & 4Sephardim Projects
(Percentages rounded off)

Haplo-group	International Profile	Santa Fe Project	4Sephardim Project	Difference* SF Vs . 4S
I	1%	14%	7%	+13% / +6%
Q	2%	4%	8%	+2% / +6%
T	3%	0%	1%	-3% / -2%
R1a	4%	1%	4%	-3% / 0%
E3b1 **	13%	2%	16%	-11% / +3%
R1b	13%	40%	43%	+26%/+30%
G	16%	4%	7%	-12% / -9%
J1	16%	20%	3%	+4% / -13%
J2	32%	14%	10%	-18% / -22%
			Total Difference	+45% / +45% -47% / -46%

These findings are significant because they show that both, the Santa Fe and the 4Sephardim DNA Projects have a cumulative of eight haplogroups which are higher than the International Sephardim Profile.

This table demonstrates the high percentage of Latino men with a Sephardic DNA haplogroup.

And it also demonstrates that despite differences, there is an amazing resemblance between the two Southwest DNA projects.

---

*SF = Santa Fe Project // 4S = 4Sephardim Project
**The International Profile reflects E3b1 while the Santa Fe and the 4Sephardim Project reflects E1b1. Nevertheless, they are both Sephardic DNA haplogroups.

Overview

These findings are revolutionary because science has legitimized the claims of many Latinos who believe they are of Sephardic ancestry but had not been able to prove it.

These findings prove that there are more Latino men in the Southwestern states of the USA with a Sephardic DNA than those found at an international level. My hypothesis is that we will start finding traces of these same phenomena in other parts of the United States as well as in Mexico and throughout Latin America. I say this because Spanish Jewry entered the New World and spread throughout all of the Americas as early as the 15th Century and continued doing so for centuries thereafter.

A minority of this large Latino population have made serious attempts to find records, archives and reliable genealogies that might reveal their true Jewish lineage. However, many have discovered that the Inquisitions and holocausts of histories past have greatly succeeded in destroying the majority of these documents. While records still exist, most people do not yet know how to access them and neither do they know how to decipher most of them in a proficient manner.

These findings provide a major breakthrough because we can now begin to explain how, when and where anyone with a Sephardic DNA haplogroup obtained such ancestral roots. Furthermore, we can now identify relatives we never knew existed, some of whom happen to be Jewish. Interestingly, some of the relatives, whether distant or close, are predominantly of Sephardic ancestry but there are also traces of Ashkenazi Jews with origins in Central and Eastern Europe.[61]

These findings are significant because they prove that both, the Santa Fe and the 4Sephardim DNA Projects have a cumulative of eight haplogroups that are even higher than the International Profile.

One of the most amazing findings is the fact that out of 230 test results in the Santa Fe Project, 59 are proven to be of the Cohanim High Priestly line.[62][63] The Cohen lineage does not respect one's physical stature or the color of eyes, hair or skin.[64] A little more than one in every four New Mexican Hispanics that took the DNA test proved to be of the Cohanim line. I must stress that this finding is highly unusual and not to be interpreted as the norm with all Latino men with a Sephardic ancestry. The international standard for Cohanim is much lower than this; certainly under 5% within the Sephardic as well as the Ashkenazi communities.

While the 4Sephardim DNA Project does not have high Cohanim test results, its results are more diversified across all haplogroups. This might point to the fact that there was a greater mixture of Sephardim entering South-Central Texas in the early days. On the other hand, the Santa Fe DNA Project shows a higher level of cohesion in terms of the Cohanim staying closely knit together as has been the case with most Jewish communities throughout many generations. One reason for this could be that New Mexico is the only state in the United States that experienced an official Inquisition with tentacles reaching all across the state.

Origin of Sephardic DNA Haplogroups

The major Jewish haplogroup that is transmitted directly from father to son across generations is the series of J haplogroups. In other words, there is no question that haplogroups such as J1 and J2 along with any of its derivatives come directly from Jewish men. On the other hand, most other haplogroups such as R1b have an entirely different means of transmitting ones Jewish ancestry.

For example, approximately 42% of Dutch men in the Jewish community are of the R1b haplogroup. Conversely, 60% of Spanish men have the same R1b haplogroup. In these types of cases, non-Jewish men impregnated Jewish women through marriage, sexual relations outside of marriage or rape. Very often these situations occurred during conflicts of invasion and war.[65]

In many cases, the non-Jewish man took on the faith of the Jewish woman and continued to bring up their children in a Jewish lifestyle. In other instances, the father did not participate in the Jewish faith but the mother raised the children in the Jewish faith and lifestyle.

We have evidences today that many men with a Jewish ancestry married non-Jewish women and thus transmitted their "J" DNA haplogroups to their sons. I have personally observed the historical phenomenon of the manner in which Sephardic men that migrated from Iberia and other parts of Europe entered the New World (of the Americas) and married indigenous non-Jewish women who in turn became Sephardic in faith and tradition. In an overwhelming percent of instances, many of these families went underground and became "Crypto-Jews" (Jews in hiding) due to the Mexican Inquisition which lasted approximately 300 years, from the early 16th Century until it was abolished in 1821/2 when Mexico finally freed itself from Spanish rule. Such Inquisitions existed in most if not all Latin American countries and islands of the Caribbean such as Puerto Rico and Cuba.

We have discovered that even though one of the parents was of Jewish ancestry and the other one was not, many Sephardic customs, practices, traditions and dialectical terms were passed on from generation to generation. However, as noted before, due to Inquisitions and a host of anti-Semitic persecutions, Sephardic Jews in the Americas went underground for survival and became what's known today as "Crypto-Jews." These Jews were formally known as *Marranos*, (swine or pigs). This was due to the fact that after Sephardic Jews were forced to convert to Roman Catholicism they were then referred to as *Marranos* and forced to eat pork.

It is significant to state that in some instances DNA results reveal exact matches with Ashkenazi Jewish men. In other words, some of the men taking the DNA test believed they were Sephardic when, in fact, they were Ashkenazi in terms of heredity but Sephardic in terms of socio-cultural upbringing. The important matter is that there is a massive awakening among Latinos who are rediscovering their Jewish ancestry through history, genealogy, material evidences, oral histories, DNA as well as onomastics which is the topic of the next chapter.

Chapter Five – Onomastic Evidences

Although the term, "onomastic" is unknown to many people, it has existed since the first name was placed on man.[66] It goes back to Genesis when Adam and Eve were first named. I say this because according to most dictionaries, the term, "onomastic" comes from the word "onomatopoeia" which means "The formation of a name or word by imitating sound associated with the thing designated." In other words, it implicates the making of words. It is my personal assessment that this field is a refined combination of both art and science due to the methods applied in the construction of names.

My aim is to provide a basis for determining if, in fact, a certain Spanish surname[67] might be of a Sephardic Jewish origin.

During the 24th International Conference on Jewish Genealogy held in Jerusalem, July 2004, I had the pleasure of meeting with a man whom I believe is today's foremost expert on Sephardic surnames, Guilherme Faiguenboim of Brazil. He was the primary reason why I had to be at this conference to hear his presentation on Sephardic surnames and to personally converse with him about certain vital questions I had regarding this subject.

My main question to him was, "When did Jewish names change from Hebrew to Spanish surnames of Sephardic origin?" His reply was that no one actually knows when this took place. One reason was due to rampant illiteracy during the medieval times leading to the Spanish Inquisition. The other reason was because by the time they laid hands on records and archives, this was all they found, namely, Sephardic surnames with Spanish sounds and construction. The names they observed were already of a Spanish intonation with a Sephardic origin.

As a result, I was able to obtain from Faiguenboim a most impressive dictionary of Sephardic surnames.[68] The three main contributing writers are: Guilherme Faiguenboim, Paulo Valadares and Anna Rosa Campagnano, all from Brazil. The dictionary was published in Brazil in 2004 and is in both English and Portuguese.

The dictionary deals with forms and variations, transliterations and alphabets as well as cultural and social criteria of Sephardic onomastics. The reliability of this dictionary is of the highest standard because it is based on 334 different data sources covering a 600 year period from the 14th to the 20th Century. It represents almost a totality of countries, regions and settlements where the presence of Sephardic communities was registered at some point throughout this 600 year period. What enhances this dictionary in a scholarly way is that the authors gleaned from and expanded on Alexander Beider's classical work titled, *Dictionary of Jewish Surnames* from the Russian Empire. Faiguenboim and associates state that the Beider "Stamped a scientific label on a subject always treated as a simple oddity and became a mandatory reference for all Jewish linguists and genealogists."

What makes this dictionary (which is more of an encyclopedia) most functional is that Sephardic names are associated to historical references such as those directly applied to the Inquisition as well as to historical personalities that were famous during that time.

Name Classification

There are eight classifications of Sephardic surnames, according to Faiguenboim and associates. I will first list them and then give a general description. They are: toponymic, patronymic, occupational, personal characteristics, artificial, biblical reference, compound and names with rabbinical origins.

Toponymic surnames have to do with geographical points such as cities, regions and countries. Among all eight classifications, this is the largest category constituting 24% of all Sephardic names. Among them are Toledano (for Toledo) and Villarreal (for villa).

Patronymic surnames are actual names placed on men from a man's proper name. This constitutes 5% of all Sephardic surnames. Some of these names are Hebrew, Spanish, Arabic, Berber (North African tribes), Portuguese, Italian, Ladino, Greek, Dutch and Basque (northern Spain/southern France). Among them are Enriquez[69] and Martinez (for Martin).

Occupational surnames relate to commerce as well as to some professional or occupational status. These constitute 11% of all Sephardic surnames. Among them are Calderon (for pots and pans manufacturer) and Molina (for mill worker or miller).

Personal characteristic surnames relate to the physical characteristics, family, housing, origin and social characteristics. These surnames constitute 21% of all Sephardic surnames. Among them are Caballero (for horseman) and Arespin (for curly hair).

Artificial surnames basically mean they have no connection with the origin or characteristics of the people who use them. For example they refer to colors, plants, animals, Catholic inspiration and others. These constitute 10% of Sephardic surnames. Among them are Lobo (for wolf), Lobato (for little wolf), Cardoso (for a plant) and Flores (for flowers).

Biblical references are those names that represent the patriarchs, kings and prophets. These names represent 9% of Sephardic names. However, it is my strong opinion that many Sephardic Crypto Jews often gave their children the first name of a Biblical character such as

Abraham, Moses, David, Solomon, Jeremiah and so forth. Among them are Gabriel (God's hero) and Abravanel (affectionate for Abraham).

Compound surnames include more than one name making up one surname such Rodriguez Pereira, de la Puente, de la Fuentes, de Leon, del Valle, Ha Levy and so on. These constitute 20% of Sephardic surnames. Among them are Núñez Lopez and de la Peña.

Rabbinical surnames include Cohen and Levy. For instance, Cohen relates directly to the first High Priest of Israel, namely Aaron, Moses' elder brother. Cohanim is also written with a "K" such as Kohanim. Levy represents the Tribe of Levi from which we get the Levites or priests and ministers of the Temple. Interestingly, in Spanish the surname Cano represents the term Cohen.[70] And the name Leyva or Leiva[71] represent Levy or Levi. The Sephardic Latino historian, Richard Santos states that there is a connection between Santos, Sánchez, Sáenz and Santellano in terms of their relationship with Jewish priesthood because their root relates to the term, *santo* as in holy. Among these names are Levi de Leon and Cohen de Lara.

Linguistic Origins

The origin of Sephardic surnames is as diverse as the names themselves. There are six different countries that are represented among Sephardic surnames. In other words, Sephardic surnames tend to emerge from the many regions where they fled or migrated 500 to 1000 years ago or more. In fact, some of these names might reflect the nations from which they were expelled or to which they fled to prior to the destruction of the Second Temple in 70 C.E.

Interestingly, the majority of Sephardic surnames reflect the very countries where Jews dwelled or were expelled to or from. For example, 39% of Sephardic surnames reflect a Spanish or Portuguese origin. After all, Jews dwelled in the Iberian Peninsula of Spain and Portugal well over a thousand years before their expulsion.

Out From Hiding

The second most significant origin of surnames is Hebrew. This represents 19% of Sephardic surnames. Here again we see how many Sephardic Anusim give Biblical names to their children, both to males and females. Among them are names of the patriarchs, kings and prophets as well as matriarchs such as Sarah, Rachel, Rebecca and Naomi.

The third most popular surname is Italian (which is Roman in its base) and represents 18% of Sephardic surnames. These are surnames which literally portray a Romanesque intonation such as Romo, Roman and Romano.

The forth most popular surname are related to Arabs. This represents 16% of Sephardic surnames. This is explainable due to the way in which Jews and Arabs coexisted as neighbors for many centuries until the Arabs overthrew Spain and persecuted the Jews. They also persecuted them throughout most of North Africa and the Middle East.

The fifth one is of Berber origin. These are the Jews that dwelled or fled to Northern Africa such as Morocco. These represent 5% of Sephardic surnames.

The sixth one is the French derivation which represents 2%.

The seventh represents all others such as the Germans, English, Dutch, the Turks and Bulgarians with less than 1%.

Most Mentioned Sephardic Surnames

There are approximately 16,914 Sephardic surnames listed in this Brazilian project. Interestingly, neither my paternal nor maternal surnames are in the top 250 most mentioned names in their list which are Sanchez and Flores. However, they are found in the exhaustive list of Sephardic Surnames.

It is important to note that these 250 most mentioned names are a little less than 1% of the grand total of Sephardic surnames in this

Brazilian onomastic project. It is also important to note that although this research was performed in Brazil, it has universal influence on Sephardic surnames because of the comprehensive and exhaustive nature of the research.

I shall only demonstrate a sampling of 50 well known Sephardic names in the United States that are found within the 250 most mentioned names in the Dictionary of Sephardic Surnames. This sampling of names constitutes only around 20% of the 250 most mentioned Sephardic names.

Fifty Well Known Sephardic Surnames in the USA

The following names are among the most common 250 Sephardic names. I have placed a number (i.e., #1, #3, #4, #7, etc.) at the end of each series of names representing the rank in which it falls among the 250 names. Interestingly, the number one name among the 250 most common names is Leon (as in lion), also written in various forms.

León (de) / Leao / Leone / Lyon / Lion / liote – #1

Rodrigues / Rodríguez / Rodrigue / Rodric / Rodrig / Rodrique… … Roderiquez – #3

Henriques / Henriquez / Enriquez / Henrique – #4

Cardoso / Cardosa / Cardozo / Cardoza / Cardoze / Cardosso… … Cardozzo – #7

Castro (de) / De Castro / Decastro / di Castro / Crasto – #9

Perez / Peres Pinto (de) – #10

Franco / Franqo – #13

Mendes / Mendez / Mendix – #14

Out From Hiding

Pereira / Perera / Pereyra / Pereyre / Paraira / Preyra – #15

Lopes / Lopez / Lofez – #17

Costa (da) / Dacosta / Acosta – #20

Nunes / Núñez / Nunez / Nounes – #22

Fernández / Fernandez / Hernandez / Fernando / Fernan – #23

Paz (da) (de) / Pas / Pax / Depas / Depaz / Depass / De Paz…

…De Pas – #27

Dias / Diaz – #31

Navarro / Navarra / Navaro / Nabarro – #33

Errera / Ferreira / Ferreira / Erera / Ereira / Ereya / Fereira… …Fereire / Ferera – #36

Gomes / Gomez / Gommes – #37

Medina – #43

Fonseca (de) / Affonseca – #46

Alvares / Alvarez / Alves / Albarez / Albares / Alvres – #47

Silva (da) / Sylva – #55

Moreno / Morenu / Morenos / Morena / Moreninis – #56

Aguilar / Aguylar / D'Aguilar / Aguiar – #62

Campos (de) / Campus – #73

Espinoza (de) / Espinossa / Espinoza / D'Espinoza / Espinosa... ...
Spinosa / Spinoza – #81

Torres (de) / Tores / Torre (dela) – #82

Romano – #86

Zacuto / Zacutto / Zaccuto / Zacutti / Zacouto / Sacudo...

...Sacouto / Sacutto – #89

Baron / Varon / Baroun / Ben baron – #90

Calderón / Calderón / Calderón – #91

Angel / Anzhel / Anzel – #104

Vale (do) / Valle (del) / Valhe (del) / Dovalle / Du Val – #108

Oliveira / Oliveira / D'Oliveira / Oliveros / Olivera – #118

Almeida / Almeida / Almeda / D'Almeida – #129

Bueno / Boeno – #140

Mendoza / Mendoca (with Portuguese comma under c)...

...Mendonca – #149

Miranda – #150

Alcalay / Alcalai / Alcalá – #159

Vega (da, de, dela) / Veiga (da) – #166

Cordova / Cordoval / Kordova – #171

García / Garcea / Garcías / Garsia / Garacie – #172

Soriano – #178

Arias – #180

Carrasso / Carazzo / Caraso / Carasso Bey – #182

Nieto / Nietto / Netto / Neto – #189

Mesquita (de) / Amesquita / Amezqueta / Mesquite…

…Misquitt Mezquitta – #206

Chaves / Chaviz / Chayes – #220

Marcos / Marcus – #224

Martins / Martines / Martínez / Martín – #225

Gutiérrez / Gutieres / Gutiérrez / Gutiérrez / Gutierez / Guterres / Guterrez – #239

Valenca (with comma under the c) / Valencia / Valentia – #249

Villareal / Villa Real / Vila Real / Vilareal / Villareale – #250

Exception to the rule

There are some cases where the surname of a known Sephardic Anusim person does not appear in any or most of the onomastic records or genealogical data bases. Take for example the surname of *Ancira*. I happen to know of a large and successful Ancira family in Monterrey, Mexico. I'm sure they are elsewhere as well. I strongly believe there are expert genealogists that can find this surname in their volumes of information and data bases. We have DNA evidence that Ancira is, in fact, Sephardic in origin. In this particular case, the gentleman on the left (in the photo below) reveals a very popular Jewish DNA haplotype "J2." The gentleman on the right belongs to an R1b DNA haplotype. I say this simply for the purpose of stating that DNA testing is yet in a state of infancy as it pertains to genealogy and anthropology. However, every day, science and technology forge ahead with new experiments and new findings.

Juan Ancira (left) and Fidel Martinez

In closing this chapter, I do not want to imply that every single person with a Sephardic/Spanish surname is, in fact, Sephardic. This can only be ascertained through DNA testing, genealogical records and archives and other methods of inquiry. Many self proclaimed Sephardic

Anusim Jews are so by choice and not by heritage or DNA. Nevertheless, as we have witnessed in this chapter that we are discovering many evidences of Sephardic bloodlines among Latinos in America; and most possibly across Latin America as well.

Chapter Six – Personal Evidences

Oral Histories[72]

Up to this point I have dealt with various arenas of evidences ranging from history to origins of names; from material evidences to the scientific evidences of DNA. However, this chapter attempts to pull it all together into a vignette format of personal evidences which can be seen as "socio-cultural case studies."

Very often, oral histories are looked down at in comparison to the documented record. However, I remind the reader that all history has come down the historical pipeline through first hand eye-witness accounts or secondary and tertiary sources of information gathering.

In this particular case, I choose to see each contributor as a court would see an eye-witness prepared to testify before the judge and jury. In other words, the testimony of a witness stands in a court of law.

In my specific case, I have served as a dynamic participant observer. My role has been similar to that of Professor Orlando Fals Borda, a Columbian sociologist, who performed what he coined to be "participatory action research." I say this in supreme professional integrity because I have taken my training and experiences into the scenes where people live and work, where they worship and play. I have learned from them, in some cases, probably more than they have from me. I have not slipped in and rushed out having received much and given little as many others have done. I have not only respected but also protected the dignity and sacredness of being ushered into people's lives, their homes and communities.

There have been hundreds of instances when I have broken bread (or tortillas) with them and shared stories that made us both weep as well as rejoice. I have been touched deep in heart with their experiences. There are some cases where, after sharing most intimate stories with my wife and me, a person would then implore us never to mention their name for fear of anti-Semitic repercussions. This is why I am indebted to each contributor of the stories I am about to share with you in the pages below.

Rachel Garcia's Story
Montana, USA

Rachel Garcia

I wish to title my abbreviated oral history: *My Journey–from home to home.*

My journey home (back to my Sephardic family and roots) started in September 1964. I was born to a Latino family in a Westside barrio of San Antonio, Texas. There, a "Jewish soul" hidden as a Hispanic female came to search her way back to her people. Hi, my name is Rachel *bat* Sarah and this is my story.

Growing up in a wonderful Christian home couldn't have been better. My parents' instruction in keeping God's Law was impeccable. We were brought up to follow God's way in joy and without reproach. Though there was something odd about us. We didn't dress the same. We didn't act the same. And we certainly didn't celebrate holidays the same. Matter of fact we didn't even celebrate Christmas or Easter at all. "Was this easy," you ask? My response: "Of course not."

"Aren't all Christians the same? Don't we all believe the same? Why are we different?" As a child, I always had questions of religion, philosophy, theology and issues of life. But none of these mean as much to me as agreeing to give each other space to live according to our personal differences and to accept the fact that some of us just don't seem to fit in just any crowd.

So, what is a child to do? For me, my safe place was my maternal grandparent's home. My grandfather Juan Olmo-Morales and my grandmother Eliza Elizondo-Sanchez de Olmo-Morales, both of blessed memory, were the foundational rock in my life.

I can still smell the Sanka coffee or Ovaltine chocolate that was served right before bedtime prayers along with whole-wheat bread and margarine spread. We sat around the small enamel-top table and quietly enjoyed the warmth of our cup in our hands. Then we proceeded to join my grandfather Juan at his bedside as we sang a few songs and recited Psalm 91 and prayed. My grandfather was very devout student of the Tanakh (the Old Testament) and giant of a spiritual man.

On one occasion my grandfather asked if my sister Neida and I had learned any new songs during our trips to Mexico. We remembered that we had learned a few of them so he asked us to sing him our new song. My bed-ridden grandfather forced himself to sit up with the help of my grandmother. While we sang, I noticed his teary eyes and he had us sing this song over and over again. At that time I had no clue why he was crying. Now I know. The song was *Aveinu Shalom Alechem*. It must have hit a deep cord in his precious Jewish soul which stirred him up and made him weep.

My mother, Sarah *bat* Eliza, told me of a story which was shared by Grandpa Juan regarding his childhood. He told her that when he was knee-high to a Mitzrayim Grasshopper and hungrier than B'nei *Ysrael in the desert*, one day he stole a piece of the bread from the cooling rack. His aunt caught him in the kitchen indulging in such a sin was madder than Pharaoh at the edge of the Red Sea. Needless to say, he went to bed that evening without supper. The moral of the story is simple—don't steal.

So, we ask ourselves, why the severity of the punishment? He was just a small child. What was so harmful about taking a piece of bread? The answer was that it was *Challah* bread, a special Jewish bread eaten every Sabbath, not just any bread. It was to be set at the table for an offering unto HaShem. He had robbed not just from his aunt but from HaShem.

Meals in their home weren't anything fancy or rich, but they were consistent and above all they were kosher. Up until this day, it seems like I can walk up and down the aisles of the HEB grocery store by my grandmother's side with her grocery list in hand. I remember the main items on her list: whole chicken, salmon, carrots, cabbage, onions, celery, peas, garbanzo beans, grapefruit juice, orange juice, whole wheat bread, Sanka, Ovaltine, milk, eggs, margarine—never a piece of pork or unclean fish.

One of my uncles is said to have blurted out one morning, "We should have bacon for breakfast," because he had tasted bacon at a friend's house. My grandpa was appalled at the idea and made a definite declaration that his home would never serve unclean food nor would it be eaten by any member of his family—ever.

My mother has shared with me how my grandpa had the custom of wearing a scarf with fringes every time he went to church. So we ask ourselves could this have been a disguise for a talit or an alternate prayer shawl. These are just a few of the memories that point to my maternal Sephardic ancestry.

I must say that surnames say much more than we think. The maiden name of Grandpa Juan's mother was Olmo-Pinedo and both are found to be Jewish. His father's surname was Morales-Torres— both found to be Sephardic. My mom went to Puerto Rico to experience the land of her father in 1994/1995. One of my grandpa's cousins told her, "Our ancestry is special and peculiar. *Somos gente real*–("We're of royal ancestry.") Don't ever forget it."

It seems I come across some of the Kabala traditions on my father's side. I can identify my grandmother Antonia doing similar things as is practiced by believers in Kabala. Of course, we called these ladies, *curanderas* (which are unconventional folk healers). My grandmother grew up with all of those traditions, she let go of it all when she became a Protestant, for it was believed to be witchcraft. Interestingly, my father's DNA came out to be Semitic. All of his surnames are found to be Sephardic as well.

A few members of my extended family have been investigating our genealogy as well as hidden secrets pertaining to our forefathers since 1996. I have discovered that this is a work only for the tenacious because of the complexities and mysteries that make this investigative journey so difficult to follow but this shall not stop me.

About two years after the discovery of my Sephardic roots, we began celebrating Chanukah. The story of Chanukah portrays my people's plight very well because of the way in which we have had to persevere against all odds as the Jewish Maccabee warriors did two millennia ago.

Their victory was in returning to HaShem after being forced to convert and Hellenized by a Grecian/pagan religion. Their journey was short but ours has lasted over 500 years—nonetheless we are and continue to be Sephardic Anusim.

After our first Chanukah celebration, we started to keep all the Feasts of the Lord, including Shabbat. We also began to keep a kosher diet. Not long after we started practicing our Jewish roots, then came the whispering and rumoring that we had turned our face away from the Messiah's grace. We were ridiculed for the accusations that we had "returned to bondage"(of the Law). These accusations and ridicule came from some family members as well as friends and acquaintances.

In my opinion, this is not half the battle. We are also looked down by B'nei Israel (the people of Israel). The red tape of rabbinic law makes it extremely difficult for us to return without conversion. And even after conversion via bona fide rabbis, the rabbinical red tape is still there to hound us. So it is that we are caught between two religions, two peoples, two worlds.

Our desire to return to our Jewish people will not be extinguished by hardship. Jewish people are tenacious because it is within our blood. We will never give up. We are determined that one day we shall be formally recognized by Israel. In the meantime we are learning Hebrew and studying Torah and observing the Feasts. My husband prays with a Minyan (of ten or more men). We regularly attend a synagogue and participate in Jewish events. After all, our journey has just begun.

Our journey home will only be complete the day we make Aliyah. Shalom.

Author's Note: Rachel's aunt once told me that her mother had an adamant passion against Catholic clerics because of the remnant behaviors of the Inquisitions and oppression of their Jewish people.

Dell F. Sanchez, Ph.D.

Bernadette Martinez' Story
New Mexico, USA

Bernadette Martinez

This is the Romero/Robledo/Gomez/Roybal y Torrado/Rael de Aguilar story. I am the oldest of seven children. My father is Cipriano Martinez and my mother was Amelia Mary Medrano. My father grew up in the Pojoaque Valley, an area located fifteen miles north of Santa Fe, New Mexico. His mother's family had been in the valley for many generations. His father grew up in Pecos, a small community east of Santa Fe, and after marrying my grandmother, they moved to Pojoaque to farm and raise their family. His name was Jose Sena Martinez and my grandmother was Ana Maria Atocha Romero.

My mother grew up in Santa Fe. Her father, Tomas Medrano, was born in Santa Fe and had been there for many generations. My grandmother, Esther Lucero, was born in Mogote, Colorado and moved to Santa Fe, in a covered wagon with her family when she was a young girl.

I also grew up in the Pojoaque Valley. This predominately Catholic Hispanic community focused on family, church and basketball! Community events took place at the Catholic Church and the winter was consumed with following the local High School basketball team. The families in this tight-knit community had been in this valley for as long as they could remember.

Other than the Native Americans from the surrounding Pueblos and a few Anglo families, we were not exposed to non-Hispanic Catholic people. It was a very secure environment and the children of the Valley were able to thrive and excel in church, school and sports.

While I was in Junior High School our librarian, Rosina Lopez, took an interest in me because I was a voracious reader. A topic that fascinated me was the history of Israel and the Jews. I began to read everything I could get my hands on. Books by Leon Uris, James Michener, Herman Wouk and others. By the time I was out of High School I had read about Ben Gurion, Golda Meir and later Moshe Dayan. By this time I had also left the Catholic Church and was attending a Bible teaching church where I could not get enough of the Old Testament.

During my first semester in college the two significant essays I wrote in my English class had to do with the fallacy of the Catholic Church and the Russian pogroms. I had no idea why I was so drawn to Israel and to the Jewish people but what I did know was that it had become a passion. This was in the early 1970's and international travel was not easy, especially for a small town girl who did not make much money. I never dreamed it would be possible to go to Israel. So instead, I just read and studied.

Dell F. Sanchez, Ph.D.

In the late 1980's I was working full time as a Vice President for a local bank while also completing my accounting degree at the University. It was at this time that the first of three pivotal events took place in my life. I happened to attend a church service in a church I infrequently visited and heard that they were taking a group to Israel. I mentioned the trip to a friend who strongly encouraged me to do whatever I had to do to go on this trip. I borrowed the money, was able to take time off work and school and could not believe that I was going to go to Israel!

The trip was life changing as I traveled to places I had only read about, as I sat on the shores of the Sea of Galilee with the water sparkling from the light of the full moon and the contour of the hills in the background. Walking through Jerusalem's Old City and making my way to the Western (Wailing) Wall was overwhelming and standing at the Mount of Olives overlooking the Temple Mount and seeing the sealed East Gate was breathtaking. It is hard to describe what this did to me except to say that when I returned home I cried for three days and knew that my life had changed. This was the first of over twenty trips I have made to Israel thus far.

I had never thought of myself as anything other than a Hispanic woman. I had wondered where we were from and how long had we been in New Mexico but did not think there was any way to trace where we came from. I do remember just after High School a classmate at the University had mentioned to me that many of the old churches in northern New Mexico had Jewish symbols carved in the woodwork. I thought that was interesting but did not equate it to the possibility that there were Jewish people involved in building these churches.

In the late 1990's I attended a workshop at a conference in Albuquerque on *Crypto Jews in New Mexico*. I was amazed to hear about the old Hispanic families, mostly from northern New Mexico, who had family traditions which appeared to have a Jewish foundation, such as lighting candles on Friday, covering mirrors when a family member passed away and not eating pork. As I heard about these traditions I mentally checked each one off–it did not appear my family had a Jewish heritage. The only one I could not be certain of was circumcision. Were the older generations of men in my family circumcised? There was only one person I could ask, so the next morning at breakfast with my grandmother, my mom and my sisters I cleared my throat and looked at my grandmother and asked, "Grandma can I ask you a question?" She responded, "Mihita, you can ask me anything you want." So I explained to her that it was a little personal but she assured me that I could ask her anything. So I asked, "Grandma was grandpa circumcised?" The shocked look on her face was worth a thousand words! She cleared her throat, pressed her lips together, and said "no," So I cleared my throat again and cautiously told her that I had one more question, and she tersely responded, "what is it." So I took a deep breath and asked, "Was his father circumcised?" She looked at me in shock and quickly responded with, "now, how would I know!" So that was that–it appeared that we did not have a Jewish heritage–yet this thing about Israel still burned in my soul.

In the mid 2000's, my brother Andrew called me. He and my aunt Elvira Martinez had been working on the Martinez genealogy. He asked if I thought we were descendants of Jews. I laughed and told him the story of the breakfast with grandma. As far as I could tell we did not have a Jewish heritage. He told me of a man he had heard on a TV program, Dr. Dell Sanchez, who talked about how many of the original Spaniards were *Conversos* coming to the New World to escape the Spanish Inquisition. He then informed me that he had invited Dr. Sanchez to speak in Santa Fe and that Dell and his wife, Helen, would be staying at my house for the next week. This was the beginning of the next pivotal event which changed my life.

As I listened to Dell's presentation I kept thinking that there was no way to find out if this was true of our family. How would we ever know if we were the descendants of the *Benei* (the people of Sephardic) *Anusim*, those who were forced to convert. Were we the *Anusim*, the descendants of those who were forced to convert? As I visited with Dell, although I had the passion for Israel and the Israeli people, I refused to embrace that I might be a *Benei Anusim*. My words to Dell were, "God will have to show this to me, I refuse to jump on the bandwagon."

Dell F. Sanchez, Ph.D.

Shortly after Dell and Helen left my home, the local media began to speak about a book which had just been published. It was by Dr. Stan Hordes called *To the Ends of the Earth, Crypto Jews in New Mexico*. I immediately went out and purchased the book. I was fascinated by the stories of some of the original colonists in New Mexico, but the names did not mean much. One evening as I was reading the book a name stuck out. So I went to our family genealogy book, written by a distant cousin, and began to thumb through it when I was struck by a name, in fact, it was the name where her study stopped. I grabbed Stan Hordes' book and looked for that name and sure enough there it was, Ygnacio de Roybal y Torrado. Where my cousin had left off, Stan Hordes picked up and took the genealogy right into Spain. All of a sudden, all the blanks started to fill in. I could not believe what I was reading. Not only were we the descendants of *Conversos*, but we were tied into many of the original colonial families of New Mexico.

The most amazing thing was that according to Dr. Hordes, Ygnacio de Roybal y Torrado, who married Francisca Gomez Robledo, were descendants of *Conversos*, was the recipient of the Jacona Land Grant. He was the father of most of the people in the Pojoaque Valley in northern New Mexico. They were his descendants. How incredible was that. Here was a whole valley of people who were *Benei Anusim*. Shortly thereafter we met a genealogist, Henrietta Martinez Christmas, who helped us put together our genealogy books for both the Martinez and Medrano families. The ties and the crossovers between the families were amazing. And to find out that many of our ancestors were from predominately Jewish communities in Spain such as Toledo, Sevilla, the Canary Islands and Portugal was overwhelming.

We also had ancestors who were tried in the Mexican Inquisition. Later, through a Catholic priest, Bill Sanchez, we were able to establish through DNA testing our Jewish lineage. My brother Andrew and I spent hours on the phone excitedly discussing the new information we were discovering about our ancestors. Eventually we were able to complete our genealogy books, "Martinez y Romero, 400 Years" and *Antepasados de Los Medranos y Los Luceros*. The next time Dell asked me if I thought we were "Benei Anusim," I was able to answer with a definite yes.

There is so much more I could share about my colonial ancestors. But this is not just my story, it is the story of many of the original families and their descendants of central and northern New Mexico. But more important than finding out who we are is realizing the truth of Scriptural prophecies. As I read in Ezekiel, Zechariah, Jeremiah, Isaiah and the other Old Testament prophets, what the God of Abraham, Isaac and Jacob has said: *Then they shall know that I am the Lord their God, because I sent them into exile among the nations and then assembled them into their own land. I will leave none of them remaining among the nations anymore. And I will not hide my face anymore from them, when I pour out my Spirit upon the house of Israel, declares the Lord God, (Ezekiel 39:28-29)*. I realize that this journey was not the product of an inquisitive mind or a searching heart, but it is the testimony of a living God who will accomplish all that He said he will do.

William E. Sanchez' Story
New Mexico, USA

William E. Sanchez (left) and Dell F. Sanchez

Now the word of HaShem came to me, saying, 'Before I formed you in the belly I knew you, and before you came out of the womb I did set you apart...
Yirmeyahu 1:4-5

Yo Soy Quien Soy

(I am who I am)

My Hebrew name is Eleazar Ben Eloi Benerito. Among the many genealogy books as well as transcribed church and governmental records that fit snugly on the shelves that stack to the ceiling of my study, one book is the most valuable and most telling of my ancestry and my destiny. It is a blue, softly padded book simply titled, *Welcome to Our Baby*.

Out From Hiding

While still in my mother's womb, she and my father, Benny, prepared carefully for their first born. It was 1953 in their first home as a married couple and a long way from my parent's ancestral lands and rivers of *Nuevo Mexico* (New Mexico). For at least three hundred years, and for some of their Native ancestors even centuries more, their families thrived on faith, family and hope for the generations to come. On page thirty-four of the worn out baby book, there is a drawing of a sturdy oak tree with broad reaching branches. On each branch is a rectangular box with a degree of relationships such as father, mother, grandfather, great grand mother, great, great grandfather, etc. In each of the branches of the family tree, my mother's graceful handwriting filled every space with the name of that ancestor: Adolfo Sanchez, Ignacita Sais, Aurelio Maestas, Nicolasa Chaves, Porfila Lucero, Juanita Nieto, Juan Lazaro Sanchez, Pabla Martines, Gabriel Chaves, Narcisso Sais, Claro Maestas and Juana Lucero. It would be decades before I continued discovering the generations further back in time and eventually entered into their deepest origins mapping their migrations and DNA Haplogroups– mostly J1's and J2's which match the priestly sons of Aaron in the Bible. These are of the Tribe of Levi, and Semites embracing the traditions and culture of *Nuevo Mexico's* Crypto Sephardic people that would be revealed to me each succeeding year of my life's journey.

My loving mother left us suddenly in August of 2000, leaving my father Benny, my two sisters, nieces and me to slowly heal our family core without the 'heart' of our lives. Added to the grieving for our mother, we were challenged with my father's cancer slowly debilitating him, though his inner strength and faith never wavered, we soon developed a plan of care and presence with him. A month before my father died in 2003, on my fiftieth year, one quiet afternoon he and I sat together in the den of our Santa Fe home intimately chatting. My father shared with me an event that occurred in San Francisco, California the very year I was born in 1953.

My father began telling me:

> *One afternoon like today, as I sat in the student lounge at the University of San Francisco, studying for my next class;*

>*an elderly, bearded man came and sat right next to me. As I glanced up from my text book, I was suddenly face to face with this stranger who stared directly into my eyes and started speaking to me what I thought to be Hebrew. All I could do was look back in response, when he blurted out, "Why are denying that you are Jewish?" I stuttered, "I am a Catholic." He retorted, "You are Sephardic, a Spanish Jew, and do not ever deny it." He was right, you know, we can never deny it.*

A few weeks later, while I was at work in Albuquerque and my sister Diane cared for my father, she called me, and began to quickly whisper. I said, "What is wrong, is it Dad?" Diane told me she was just sitting with Dad in the den watching some football game when he turned to her and said: "Two more weeks, Diane, two more weeks." I asked him, "Dad, do you mean the Super Bowl? Are you saying it is in two more weeks, because it is not?" Dad said, "No Diane, you know what I mean, two more weeks."

On February the 2nd, 2003, two weeks after his announcement, Eloi Benerito (Benny) Sanchez went home quietly in the early dawn to be with God as my sister slept soundly beside him. He died in the very home he had shared with Aurora, our mother, for 49 years.

His death caused me to remember how on my first birthday, my parents had moved back to New Mexico and began a home in Santa Fe. Every Friday afternoon we would drive two hours to the parent's home of my mother in Santa Rosa and spend the weekend with them. Early in my memory, I recall my maternal grandmother, Nicolasa Chaves and Maestas, placing something in the front window of her home every December. It had seven plastic candles with seven bulbs which my grandmother would twist into place, one each evening until finally all seven electric candles glowed in the front window of her home. I remember that six of the bulbs were clear and the middle one a gentle blue. Much later in life I came to understand the December electric lights to be a Menorah that was lit in my grandmother's home to celebrate a feast that was not Christmas, it was Chanukah, a Jewish feast, not a Christian one.

The Sais family of my paternal grandmother told the children a story about *the pig that ate the baby*. The story was about a little baby that crawled out of his family's home and wandered over to a neighbor who owned a pig and the pig ate the baby. Pork never seemed appetizing remembering the pig chewing on the poor little baby. Children could never be trusted with the righteous secrets, so there were other ways to teach them an important aspect of our Crypto-Sephardic life style.

Not long ago, my father's sister phoned me and asked to come for a gift she had for the church where I pastor. I went to her home and found a rectangular box on the dinning room table that once belonged to my grandmother. She handed me the box and said,

> *This is a special table cloth that once belonged to my mother's mother, Mama Juanita Nieto y Sais. She used this table cloth for special meals in her home, and it should be used for your altar when you offer mass. Mama Juanita was your father's godmother.*

"Well, *Tia*, if this was used by my great grandmother for her table, why can't I use it for my dinning room table?" She replied, "Because it is special and sacred, not for your table in your home, but for the altar in your church." My aunt was transferring the sacredness of my great grandmother's Sabbath dinner and the beautifully weaved table cloth from her treasured past on to the present which was sacred for her now; and that it would be used for the altar table during Catholic mass.

This reminded me of the time that caused me to turn the clock of memory back before my father passed away, in 2001. He and I were watching a PBS TV special on human DNA. At the end of the program was a segment on two new companies that were now testing humans for a DNA analysis. One company was in Oxford, England, and the other in Houston, Texas. At this time, my father recommended we send for kits from both companies and compare the results of our Y-DNA of our paternal line and Mitochondrial DNA of our maternal line, and he offered to pay for them. And so I ordered the kits from the advertised DNA testing companies we sent them off, eagerly to discover our own DNA. As soon as we could we sent the DNA kits with the saliva tests to the two laboratories in England and Houston, Texas.

Three weeks later, I received a phone call from Dr. Bennett Greenspan, owner and founder of Family Tree DNA laboratory in Houston, Texas. Dr. Bennett began by asking me: "Are you William Sanchez, kit number such and so?" "Yes, I am William Sanchez and that is my kit number." "Did you know that you were Jewish," Dr. Greenspan asked. "Yes," I said, "that is our tradition." "Did you know that you were a Cohen from the priestly class of Aaron, the brother of Moses?" "No," I said, "I did not know that we are Cohen." "Well," Bennett continued, "What do you do for a living?" "I am a Catholic Priest," I said. Dr. Greenspan was quiet for a few moments and then said, "Well, we will take you back." "Well sir, we never left," I replied.

Over four hundred years ago, our Spanish Jewish ancestors were coerced by violence to become Catholic, but as *conversos* (converts) they were never recognized as equals to the Old Christians. We are the *Anusim*, those who converted not out of a sincere decision to embrace a new faith, but out of a human instinct to survive.

When the Los Angeles Times and many other major newspapers and national magazines ran articles on my DNA discoveries and my Sephardic heritage the mystery of my people's Sephardic roots hit the public. What was once hidden is now out in the open for everyone to see. Some reflected on their own Sephardic journey and responded in a variety of ways.

What has been most surprising have been the times when I have been angrily confronted by others who were anti-Semitic. The worst of those whom I have been confronted by usually begin with the 'lie about the Holocaust,' others are critical that I would bring out the violence of the Spanish Inquisition, or the call by Martin Luther for his followers to burn Torahs and Synagogues.

Recently, a man from the New Mexico Hispanic Culture Preservation League publicly stated that the "New Mexico Crypto-Jews were a fantasy." And he angrily told me that what I was doing was nothing more than erroneous propaganda.

On a more profound level, I personally find it very painful to proclaim a gospel within the church that blames the Jews for killing Jesus. Something in the pit of my stomach tightens when I have to read the Gospel Passions out loud and each year during Holy Week, hear the mob of Jews screaming "crucify him, crucify him!" Sometimes I think of taking my vacation during Holy Week and returning after Easter. I fear that such a Christian gospel inspired the many violent pogroms that massacred so many of my Jewish ancestors and quite possibly could still become the cause of my own death today.

My first visit (or return) to Jerusalem, since my Cohen ancestors left in 587 BCE and journeyed to Sefarad (Iberia-Spain), was truly an overwhelming experience for me. I can honestly say that I have never felt so at home as I felt being in Jerusalem and Israel. I never wanted to leave again; and if possible I would love to some day make Aliyah and become an Israeli citizen. This would be a dream come true—my journey completed.

Dell F. Sanchez, Ph.D.

Arnella Martinez' Story
Texas, USA

Arnella Martinez with Husband Orlando

One spring night in 1996, my Dad came home real excited but with noticeable skepticism about a family secret his Dad has just told him. This secret had been kept from my grandfather for 77 years and finally his contemporary nieces broke silence and told him what their mothers demanded they never repeat.

This family secret had been kept airtight for almost a century while grandfather's sisters knew most of the story and his brothers only knew bits and pieces of it. The secret was that grandfather's father (my great grandfather Delfino I) had been given up for adoption by an officer in the Mexican Military who happened to be a *Judio* (a Jew).

But to my knowledge, my family story doesn't really start here; it actually begins with Mom telling us that she was "Jewish" on her mother's side—so I'll get back to Dad's story later.

I remember Mom telling me that she had Jewish roots on her mother's paternal side—the Martinez family. She declared to us that this was common knowledge within their entire extended family. However, she also said that their family customs and traditions were demonstrated more as familial and cultural rather than Jewish. While growing up, they lived in a Jewish community in Denver, Colorado, yet they never practiced the orthodoxy of their Jewish neighbors. They lived more as Crypto-Jews, never telling outsiders of the family secret that they were Jews—Sephardic Jews in fact.

Mom's maternal grandfather's extended family was raised in Northern New Mexico where we now have extensive evidence that most of the early pioneers of that area were Sephardic Crypto-Jews. They migrated to what's known today as Southern Colorado which is very similar to Northern New Mexico in terms of the preponderance of Sephardic Crypto-Jews in that area.

In one of my parent's many journeys to New Mexico, Mom discovered that her Martinez family fits perfectly into another Martinez family tree of Northern New Mexico. These New Mexican Sephardic Jews have traced their paternal and maternal genealogies all the way back to the first pioneers and leaders of New Mexico. In fact, they entered New Mexico with a famous Sephardic Conquistador named Don Juan de Oñate.

Just a few days ago, after Mom's younger brother took a DNA test through the Family Tree DNA laboratory in Houston, Texas and we were stunned with a very peculiar story. Initial lab results reveal that Mom's father has one of the most popular Jewish DNA haplogroups. Further analysis will be administered because of the probability that Mom's father was of the Cohen line which is of the High Priestly order of Aaron, Moses' older brother. I'm referring to Moses in the Bible during the great Exodus. I've always wondered about Mom's father because he seemed so different. Now I know!

On the other hand, my Dad's paternal line has a very peculiar DNA which isn't very surprising to most of our Sanchez family members because they seem different to most all other Sephardic Hispanics. They just don't fit the general mold as a Hispanic family. But now I know why this is so.

What's very interesting is that Dad's and Mom's maternal grandfathers share the same DNA; but they come from two different areas of the Southwest and are not related. In other words, they're of a Sephardic extraction. While Dad and Mom's paternal sides have a different DNA, yet, they appear to emerge from the same parts of Central and Eastern Europe which seems strange to me. In other words, how did our forefathers come from such a distant region of the world, bringing their Jewish traditions and secrets and never giving up despite all those Inquisitions, Pogroms and anti-Semitic assaults?

I confess that DNA testing is a new frontier in terms of ascertaining one's Jewish ancestry; but we do have other reliable sources of information. Sadly we don't have more knowledge published on these subjects; but, we cling to the vestiges of oral histories which have continued to linger among our people and especially our elders. I'm proud to have known my Dad's parents and Mom's father who are now deceased, blessed be their memory. Nonetheless, at this very time we have five generations that come together under one roof in my mother's side. These include my maternal grandmother (age 96), my mother, my sister, her daughter and her grand daughter. We're rich with oral histories and traditions on all sides of our family tree.

Having said this and because we know much less of Dad's family than we do of Mom's side, I wish to continue my story with Dad's family—not because it's more important but because it is **as** important as anyone else's (but my parents' histories are more important to me because I'm in this huge trans-generational family portrait).

Dad's discovery of his Sephardic Jewish ancestry exploded like a bombshell in our home in '96. This catapulted not only Dad but also Mom into a lifetime of investigation. They knew deep in their souls that they weren't doing this merely for themselves but for untold thousands of others just like them scattered across our Western Hemisphere. They traveled to so many major libraries across the Southwest of the USA. They even traveled to Mexican archive centers and met with archivists and historians across America and Mexico. They even traveled twice to Spain in their quest to discover the truth to their most intimate ancestral questions. In their fervor they've traveled to Israel around 30 times since '96. They've developed relationships with Israeli leaders in academia, science, government as well as the religious sector. Their dream has been to see a community in the Negev particularly for people like themselves who've recently emerged from the ash heaps of history's past.

In the midst of their odyssey, they've pulled together pieces of Dad's ancestral puzzle. One thing they discovered was that the archival records pertaining to Dad's paternal grandfather have completely disappeared from the institutions that are supposed to guard them. Those records are gone and nowhere to be found in the province of his birth as well as in Mexico City's national records and other well known archival centers in America. I ask, "What was so peculiar or so threatening to the 'powers that be' about Dad's grandfather's generation of the mid to late 1800's in Montemorelos and much of northern Mexico?" In the process they discovered that many of those records were destroyed in order to conceal certain secrets of that particular era in Mexico.

After a brisk historical investigation, we've discovered that the socio-political scene in Mexico was extremely volatile in the late 1800's. In fact, just two to three years before grandfather Delfino I was born to the alleged officer in Maximillian's army, his top ranking officers and other soldiers were executed after Benito Juarez took the reigns over Mexico. We've also discovered that many of his soldiers were imprisoned and others fled the country, some of whom landed in New Orleans. We do not know but I ask, "Could grandfather Delfino's father have been one of those in flight or imprisoned or later executed?" We just do not know.

Slowly this ancestral puzzle began to take shape, although there's still 'a ton' of investigation needed in order to see the big picture more accurately. Thanks to the fact that Dad's paternal family did a good job of hiding and preserving ancient secrets that pertain to their Sephardic roots. Thank God that Dad and a few of his siblings and cousins (but mostly Dad and Mom) began to desperately dig for truth whiles their aged parents and extended family members were still alive and able to tell the secret stories of whom they really were.

In keeping with Sephardic tradition, the adoptive parents placed great grandfather Delfino in a Catholic monastery. The rationale for this tradition was simply to keep the Roman Catholic Inquisitors and spies off their backs. The Roman Catholic Inquisition was determined to erase all vestige of Jewishness from the heart and soul of these Sephardic individuals; therefore, they took the first born son of each Sephardic family and placed him in a monastery to be trained for the priesthood. This way they could not only keep a better eye on their Sephardic *conversos* that might begin to Judaize but also to 'delete' any and all memories of Spanish Jewry from their midst. The main purpose for this was to keep guarded control over their Roman Catholic *Marranos*.

The story told to me and my siblings is that great grandfather Delfino kept escaping from the monastery. The leadership of the monastery would go find him, take him to his adoptive father, Jose Maria Sanchez at which time he was vigorously whipped by him and sent back to the monastery. His monastery superiors would then whip him and place new demands on him. However, great grandfather kept fleeing the monastery and the cycle of physical abuse (and perhaps torture?) was repeated time and again.

One day, great grandfather escaped and crossed the Rio Grande. In the process he married a Tofoya (or Tafolla) girl of the early pioneer Sephardim in Santa Fe, New Mexico. Dad has a most elaborate genealogical tree on this family and sure enough, our great grandfather on it through marriage. However, his bride died early in marriage due to poor medical science so in turn he married an Elizondo girl of the pioneers of Monterrey, Mexico. Interestingly, Santa Fe, New Mexico and Monterrey, (old) Mexico are the two most renowned hubs of the Sephardic Anusim in the New World.

Great grandfather (Delfino I) and Juanita Elizondo had a large family of about a dozen kids, the youngest of which is my grandfather, Delfino II (my father is Delfino III and my first born son is Nathaneel Delfino). Almost all of them have popular names found in the *Tanakh* (Old Testament) such as Daniel, David, Joshua and so forth. The girls' names tend to end with the phonetic sound of "ah" which points to Yah or Jah, the Name of God. They include Otila(h), Elisa(h), Delia(h) and so forth. Interestingly, Dad and Mom's sisters and aunts are also named in this fashion such as Minerva(h), Arnella(h), Cordelia(h) and so forth.

Dad tells us that his mother's family had peculiar cooking and butchering habits that weren't necessarily of Mexican culinary tradition. Of the many examples the ones that stick out in my memory best are these: when a family member passed away, they'd cover all mirrors in the house; when Dad's maternal grandfather passed away, they kept his chair vacant for some weeks and they'd do their best at giving his meal to some homeless person or a beggar; while his aunt was making flour tortillas, she would throw a tiny pebble of dough into the open fire.

Dad's mother loved Mexican sweet bread called *Pan de Semita*. He used to think it was *pan de semillita* which means bread with tiny (anise) seeds but it was actually bread of *Semita* (Semite) Jews. They often ate *empanadas* stuffed with sweet potato or pumpkin; but in the old days some would stuff their empanadas with diced meat, some veggies and raisins. Dad discovered that the flour tortilla was their Sephardic (Jewish) matzo. He also discovered that the Mexican sarape—that colorful shawl worn predominantly by men was the actual prayer shawl or talit of his people. He has even shown my siblings and me how many Mexican sombreros are designed with a large Star of David on the top.

I'd love to go on and on with this story because I feel it's more than noble memories, it represents the dignity and legacy left for us to follow and never forget the secret of who we really are.

During one of his many meetings with our rabbi, Rabbi Scheinberg of Rodfei Sholom in San Antonio, Texas, something very solemn happened to Dad, something that sealed our family's Jewishness in our hearts forever. The rabbi asked Dad, "Do you believe you're a Jew?" Dad's response was, "No sir! I don't believe—I know I am a Jew!" This settled the issue of our Jewishness as our rabbi embraced us and has made us feel a true sense of belonging, something that we've always desired to experience all our lives. Now our family is awaiting the same kind of belonging as we wait on the Israeli government's final word regarding our citizenship (Aliyah) to become one with them and to fulfill our destiny.

Rebecca Guidry's Story
Texas, USA

Photo Not Available

My name is Rebecca Ruth Sanchez Guidry. I am the youngest child of Sephardic parents. My father Delfino Sanchez Sr. first told me of my Sephardic roots in 1996. He approached me one night and teasingly told me *Mija, que Judia eres!* ("Daughter, what a Jew you are!"). I looked at him surprised. He laughed and with a twinkle in his eye repeated, "What a Jew you are." When I asked him for clarification he began to tell me a story that confirmed many things directly related to our Sephardic ancestry which had been on my heart since I was a child.

Imagine, my father being the youngest of eleven had just found out a secret that had been kept from him for seventy-seven years. As he shared what was told to him I could see the pride in his eyes and the excitement to finally know what made him special and unique.

As he shared this new story, I stood amazed that such information could remain so secretive for almost a century. This unfolding secret swept me into a very fascinating realm of intrigue and expectation.

Unbeknownst to my father, the story was that his father had been given up for adoption by Sephardic parents. All indications point to the fact that his adoptive parents were also descendent Jews from Spain. Fearing the persecution of the Inquisition that had followed their families from Spain into Mexico they chose to remain Crypto–hidden from any and all forms of Judaism. I have validated this story through records and also by getting my father to submit to a DNA test; and his test results corroborate this story I am sharing with you at this time.

Some of his older sisters and brothers knew of this secret. In fact, I believe it was Dad's older brother, Josue, who finally disclosed the truth about their father's Sephardic ancestry to one of his older sons, Efrain. Excited with the news, cousin Efrain quickly phoned my father whom he loved and respected very much. Dad immediately did a little investigation with his contemporary nieces and they seemed to have much more knowledge than the men did; probably because it was a Sephardic custom that the mothers would share the secret of their Sephardic identity with their daughters and not with their sons because sons do not keep a good secret. This opened up a brand new and exciting beginning in my life and most of my siblings.

Things have always taken time for me to absorb and embrace, thus, change has not always come very easy because of my analytical mind. At first I was happy to hear the news but through the months and years I wanted to know more. I wanted to learn more about my heritage and destiny that had been kept from me. Who really was I? Where did I belong? Did I belong in a local church or in a synagogue? Where do I begin to explore my roots?

My first and deepest impression in my new journey was visiting Israel in 2002. That trip has changed my life forever. In fact, as the plane flew into Israeli airwaves I began to weep. I was so deeply moved. I felt that I was returning home! As I ascended into Jerusalem and visited the Western (Wailing) Wall, I wept a lot. The honor of finally knowing who I was and that I was one among my extended Jewish/Israel family has continued to be an overwhelming experience for me.

In the process of my reconstructing my life's story, in an attempt to identify anything Jewish in my family, I began to capture some clues and hints that sparked within my soul. For instance, I remember being in the second or third grade and a quiet Mexican boy of olive complexion joined our class as a new student. As we paired up for art, I saw how he made his star and something inside me moved. I asked him "How did you do your star? I want to do my star like that too." It was the Star of David. Now, I am aware that under normal conditions this means absolutely nothing. However, this matter of drawing the Star of David was not a mere matter of artwork or curiosity but profound significance within my soul. I felt a connection much higher with Israel than a sincere spirit of Zionism–this connection was more a matter of life and death to my inner soul. Without this I dare say my life would have a shallow meaning to it.

I remember going to physical education class and we were to dance various styles of dances. First we danced The *Raspa* followed by "The Cotton Eye Joe." Then the teacher put on Israeli music and I must say that I kind of 'lost it' in terms of my conscious awareness of being one with a people I didn't even know, with origins on the other side of the ocean. As I danced I kept saying to myself, "Oh how wonderful." The dance came so easy to me. Almost as if I'd always danced this way since my infancy, but I hadn't. An excitement stirred within me and I didn't want the music to stop. My feelings were so moved that I didn't know how to express what was going on inside of me. I didn't know if I should laugh, cry, yell or what! It was mystical because I felt a connection of soul with the land and the people which this music represented which was Israel and her Jewish children.

Everyone in the neighborhood seemed to know we were different and my parents were highly esteemed by everyone in the community. Yet we were so different from all others around us. One day, as I walked home from school, I passed in front of a little *cantina* (saloon) and I heard a man say to another, *Son Marranos* (they're Marranos). I wondered at the young age of eight or nine why this man would call me a pig. As a child I was concerned why he chose to call my family pigs. A few years ago I discovered that the term *Marrano* was used by members and cohorts of the Inquisition to portray a Sephardic Jew who had been forced to convert to Roman Catholicism and forced to eat pork in public. These conversions were forced upon Sephardim in Spain, Portugal, Mexico and various regions of Latin America while the victim was under tremendous physical, emotional and spiritual duress. In other words, this forced conversion was administered while the victim was being tortured. In fact, many of them were burnt at the stake dead or alive in connection to this whole issue of conversion to the Roman Catholic faith.

Some of our family traditions were a little different than others even in our own Hispanic neighborhood. I remember my mother never desiring to eat any type of seafood other than tuna or fish sticks. She absolutely would not eat shrimp or shelled seafood. She had a repulsion to shrimp that seemed unusual.

Mom also had my sister and I give a thanksgiving prayer after our meals as we dismissed ourselves from the table. I asked her "Mom, why do we have to say a thanksgiving when we already prayed before the meal?" She answered, "That's the way I was taught."

One of my mom's favorite Mexican sweet bread was *Pan de Semita*. I used to think this meant *pan de semillita* which means bread containing small seeds because of all the tiny anise seeds in it. But I've recently discovered the word is not *semillita* (tiny seeds) but *Semita* which means Semite as in Jewish. She seemed to especially enjoy this bread in the springtime because of the Passover season and what it represented to us.

My father told us stories of how he and certain siblings were asked, *Son Judios?*–"Are you Jews?" Their response was *No, somos Mexicanos*–"No, we're Mexicans." Yet they would teasingly tell one another *Somos Levitas* – "We're Levites" (of the Tribe of Levi). There always seemed to be a feeling of truth to this. Now we know why; after all, my father's DNA test reveals some linkages to Levites of Eastern Europe.

Through the years I have continued to slowly walk out my heart's yearning. There have been times that I have doubted myself, thinking this is too good to be true. Now I know it was fate leading me onward all along.

Today, I can say that I have gone to Israel three times, taken a Hebrew beginner class and am learning all I can and sharing it with my daughters and my extended family. I have invested in a Siddur and the copy of the Torah. I am religious about prayer, studying Torah and the Tanakh (the Old Testament) as I continue to grow in knowledge and connectedness with my Jewish family.

My heart and mind have so changed since 1996. Today, I faithfully attend a local synagogue and take all the classes I can that are taught by the rabbis and leadership of our shul. Now, I desire to make Aliyah as soon as feasible. I desire to fulfill my destiny together with my children as Israeli citizens in the land of our inheritance which is the Negev. I do believe my children and their children will follow in my footsteps 'back home.'

Kathy Baca's Story
New Mexico, USA

Kathy Baca

My father had an engaging personality and could light up a room quite easily. I was four or five years old when I remember him asking elderly relatives a question in Spanish, and suddenly the room would become quiet. Since he was intrigued with our potential Sephardic Jewish ancestry his question sounded something like, *Somos Judios?*–(are we Jews)? His question was sincere and almost demanding to get facts about their family's history. Though he was persistent in asking, he never received a suitable response. This issue was kept very secretive so there simply was no discussion on the subject. At the end of his life, he accepted their silence as answer enough. In other words, this perpetual silence somehow showed him there was something very crucial about their past that no one really wanted to discuss.

The name given to my father at birth in 1919 was Tobias Patricio Espinosa. Eventually he changed it to Toby Patrick Espinosa so that everyone could spell and pronounce it properly. He was the son of Patrick Joseph Espinosa and Josefina Chavez of Del Norte, Colorado. He was a very bright student and was among the first Hispanic children to be integrated into the public school system in Colorado. Speaking Spanish as a first language, he soon recognized that he would have to quickly master English over the summer—and that he did.

My father's vital need to know where he came from may have been intensified by his own personal circumstances. He was one of thirteen children, some of which died in infancy and one died at six of asthma. His family had sustained a lot of losses so when the depression hit, his parents gave two children away to relatives who were in better financial shape to rear them well. So my Dad went to live with his maternal grandparents. As he grew a little older, he was sent to herd sheep far up into the Ouray Mountains. While the sheep grazed, this allowed him plenty of time to think about some of the deep issues that were persisting within him concerning the origin of his family.

Family meant everything to my father and as a married man he sought to re-establish himself with his immediate family, pursuing relationships even with third and fourth cousins. My parents were both extremely hospitable people. Though my mother was neither Hispanic nor Jewish, she certainly gave her own generous contribution to the cause. She entertained and provided comfortable beds for everyone. Preparing outstanding meals, and a welcoming spirit, Mom would encourage the relatives to stay a little longer, and the discussion of our true heritage would continue deep into the night.

In the meantime, my father was grateful for lengthy conversations with his brothers and cousins like Toby J. Espinosa. His heartfelt discussions included Uncle Henry Espinosa, who would recount the past with him over and over. Dad was a history buff and though he had no formal education, he was always studying, investigating and saturating himself with knowledge. Based on his own research, he had suspected that our family might have been one of the fortunate ones who escaped the Inquisition in Spain.

We have expanded our investigation with the assistance of relatives such as our cousin Joanne. We were very fortunate to receive from cousin Gilberto (Antonio Gilberto) Espinosa an amazing parchment that was approximately two by three feet in size. The title of this paper was *Colonists and Soldiers who accompanied Don Juan de Oñate to New Mexico in 1598 and established the first capital of New Mexico, San Gabriel.* There are approximately 135 names in this list.(*)

Appearing on that list was twenty-one year old Captain Marcelo de Espinosa, son of Antonio de Espinosa, who resided in Madrid, in the province of Castilla de Nueva. The next sighting of our surname appears in the same year that the first capital of New Mexico was established by Don Juan de Oñate in San Gabrielle on September 8, 1598. It is quite significant that this history was made available to us as a result of my grandfather's cousin, Gilberto Espinosa's book regarding the first settlers. However, much more research is needed to follow our family through the next 200 years.

During the last two years before my Dad passed away in 1977, he did something that brought great inner satisfaction which was to enroll in Hebrew School. He was perfectly content and at peace with himself after discovering the truth that is laid out in the Holy Scriptures which provides more than enough truth to live on as a distinctive people.

Continuing with Dad's quest, I began to listen a little more intently at family get-togethers. I also took note of history and research available on the subject of Sephardic Jews, acquiring a small library of books for myself. I attended a few conferences with Dr. Dell Sanchez, author of various books on the subject and effective conference speaker. I enjoyed attending the lecture series at the University of New Mexico with my cousin, Henry Espinoza as Dr. Stanley Hordes did an exceptional job in teaching the facts about our Sephardic ancestry. Dr. Hordes is New Mexico's former historian, a professor and noted expert and author on this subject. As we compared notes, I intently listened, I begin to realize the serious possibility that Dad's suspicions of our Sephardic ancestry were true. After a long series of events, I began to realize that my suspicions and debates regarding our Sephardic ancestry were beginning to swing more and more in an affirmative direction.

During a period of time, my husband and I owned a printing company; and one day a customer asked me to copy an article from a magazine called *La Herencia* (The Inheritance). Glancing down the page, I noticed a listing of people' names that had been put to death during the Spanish and the Mexican Inquisitions and our name appeared on both lists. After all these years I felt I was ready for a final word–a firm answer to my quest. So I finally spoke with my son, Damian Baca (**) about DNA testing, and within six to seven weeks we had the proof of our true identity which my dear father had been passionately searching for throughout his entire adult life.

Yes, we are the Sephardic Jews that are mentioned in the Book of Obadiah in the Holy Scriptures. I am still trying to absorb God's amazing plans for our people and I am praying for the courage to personally follow God's promises and to fulfill our destiny. God is ready to pour out blessings that will equip us to fulfill His ancient prophecies regarding our people and the Promised Land of Israel. But God is gracious enough to serve me what I need to know in small portions so that I do not get ahead nor fall far behind Him. Yet, I am thrilled for those who are dynamically fulfilling the prophecy that pertains to living in Israel and specifically in the Negev which the ancient Prophet Obadiah so clearly speaks about.

In 2006 my husband, Dan and I were given an opportunity to travel to Israel. It truly was the greatest experience of our lives. As we got off the bus in Jerusalem, I noticed the people ahead of me walking very slowly. Our line didn't seem to be moving at all, and then I noticed there was a reception line ahead with what appeared to be all of the staff of the hotel. Each employee welcomed us individually to the establishment with very kind and sincere greetings. Once I crossed the threshold of the door, my immediate thought was, I'm home. Then, flooding into my heart was the greatest sense of belonging I have ever known. I wondered how I could be at home if I'd never even been there before. But I had read stories about people making Aliyah, and returning back to their homeland. Though my experience was a completely unscheduled event, lasting for only ten glorious days, nevertheless, it felt like a real homecoming to me.

As I look at the Espinosa family today, it is easy to see that the Lord has blessed and given us favor. Despite the fact that our name was the fifth most common name of people burned at the stake in the Inquisition in Spain, out of the remnant, the Lord has allowed our family to flourish. From humble beginnings as sheepherders and ranchers, the generations that have followed have been given the opportunity to study in the field of their choosing.

Today we have several authors, teachers, engineers, lawyers, numerous professors, computer experts, principals, editors of television, business owners, social workers, a doctor, a dentist, a diplomat, a naval commander, a television producer and many who have excelled in music and the arts. This family is so large that I do not know each of them nor their varied accomplishments. Surely God has kept His hand upon them.

Our cousin, Linda Espinosa (***) arranged a family reunion for us in Pagosa Springs, Colorado in 2008. There we re-established ourselves with one entire Espinosa family that we had lost contact with over a century ago. To our surprise, they had been living in the Pagosa area for all these years. We learned more about the missing gap of time from a video made by my late Uncle Ted (Theodore) Espinosa. This re-uniting would have thrilled my Dad's heart.

My prayer is that we will take note of who we are and that God has rescued and preserved us for a destiny which is becoming clearer to me every passing day. He is the God of Abraham, Isaac and Jacob and His faithfulness continues through all generations. He has proven to us that He is the One who kept the promises He made to our ancestors. *Remember me, O Lord, when you show favor to your people, come to my aid when you save them, that I may enjoy the prosperity of your chosen ones, that I may share in the joy of your nation and join your inheritance in giving praise,* Psalm 106: 4, 5.

(*) Parchment received from Henry D. Espinosa, MBA, DDS, Periodontal Practice in Albuquerque, NM
(**) Damian P. Baca, PhD Rhetoric and Cultural Composition, University of Arizona, Tucson
(***) Linda Espinosa, PhD Early Childhood Development, University of Missouri, Columbia

Moses Orona's Story
Arizona, USA

Moses Orona

My family and I entered a Jewish bakery to purchase some Challah bread for Sabbath. The storeowner looked at us and asked, "Why are you buying this bread?" My wife told him, "To celebrate Shabbat." He stared at us in disbelief for a few seconds, then asked, "Are you Jewish? We told him, "Yes we are."

Needless to say, it caused quite a stir and everyone in the market (it was quite full at the time) gathered around us. You see I am tall with black hair and black eyes with a dark complexion. In other words I look what some consider to be "very Hispanic" and not your typical looking Jew (whatever that means). My two sons are also quite tall, dark and handsome and their mother is Spanish looking in everyway.

My wife explained to them that I had taken a DNA test and it was discovered that we are of Jewish descent. Someone in the back of the group shouted out, "It's true, I have heard of this before. They are Sephardic and are part of a great phenomenon that is happening among Hispanics." I proceeded to tell them that we also have Ashkenazi roots.

The storeowner exclaimed, "It is not possible, you must be one or the other, you cannot be both! The blood is never mixed." I looked him in the eye and said, "Nevertheless, I am both. You see my paternal grandfather was from Germany and was of Ashkenazi descent. My maternal grandfather came from Ireland. On the other hand, both of my grandmothers descended from Spain and were Sephardic. I guess our God is a part-time geneticist as well. By the way, our DNA markers came back and indicate that we have a lot of matches to Jews with Levite roots.

Suddenly, it got really quiet in that store and no one spoke. My family and I decided that it was a good time to make our get-away as we headed toward the door. But before we managed to make it out the door, a young woman called out to me and asked, "How many Sephardics are there out there?" I stopped, looked at her and said, "We are more than you'd think."

This has been a normal occurrence for me and my family since HaShem chose to reveal this secret that has been hidden from our people for over five hundred years. He even managed to place us strategically in a Jewish neighborhood surrounded by Jewish synagogues. Surely God makes no mistakes.

I cannot say that it has been easy to make all the changes that are required in the acceptance of our new heritage. Even my family has questioned our motives. Some of them fail to understand that we have chosen to pursue our Jewish roots based on our love for God and our commitment and to fulfill His ancient prophecies for us.

Many of our friends have gone so far as to call us crazy saying, "Why would you want to join a culture that is hated and despised by everyone! It is difficult enough being Hispanic, why on earth would you add to your troubles." Some sadly, have chosen to stop talking to us all together. However, we have managed to persevere and continue to grow in the knowledge that God is with us. We are never alone!

Some folks think we have known about our Sephardic roots for a long time because of the way in which we live our lives. But the fact is that this journey barely began about a year and a half ago when we met a man who had traveled from North Carolina to our state of Arizona. In good faith he sold his home and his business and transplanted his family thousands of miles to the west. He did this because of a deep, inner passion to fulfill God's purpose in his life regarding his love for Jews and Erez Israel.

He told us of his love for the Jewish people and how this had brought him to Phoenix. His wife told us of her love for Hispanics who make up a great percentage of the population here in Phoenix, Arizona. She shared with us about her desire to live among Hispanics and particularly with Hispanic/Latinos with a Jewish background.

It wasn't until Tom led us to the book of Obadiah verses 19-21 that we discovered our people's role in Israel and with our Jewish family. The verse that hit us straight between the eyes was verse 20 where it says, *and the captivity of Jerusalem which is in Sepharad shall posses the cities of the South (which is the Negev)*. Then in verse 21 it says that *liberators shall come up on mount Zion to judge the mount of Esau; and the kingdoms shall be the Lords.* This means we will enter the Promised Land as pioneers to take possession of the land our people is to inherit in the Negev.

Obadiah's Scripture quickly became the theme of our family's desire–to return to the land that God promised abba Abraham. But the most intriguing aspect of all is that we've learned that God will be orchestrating the return of the Anusim with all of his heart and soul according to the ancient Prophet Jeremiah 32, verse 40. It states, "...and I will faithfully and whole heartedly replant them in this land."

Up until my awakening from my people's slumber had I ever come across any other Scripture that refers to HaShem's desire to do something with all of his heart and soul. But this is exactly what He intends to do. My family and I can find no excuse to deny what God has asked of us.

One of the things I find most amazing as I look back on our youth is discovering the many hidden secrets that existed within our daily life–and we didn't even know they were Sephardic in origin. A few of them include the following: lighting of candles on Friday evenings; the manner in which mothers would wait forty days before appearing in public after the birth of a child; the biblical names that were given to each new infant which were specifically tied the Tanakh known as the Old Testament. One example is the very names placed on my siblings– Rachel, Jacob, Benjamin, and David. My name is *Moises* or Moses.

The patriarchs of our family did not stray far from their roots. For example, my grandfather, who was a farmer in Mesilla New Mexico, had a ranch of over 10,000 acres in which he planted cotton to make his living. For instance, on the outer edges of his farm, he planted melons, corn, and vegetables of every kind. When harvest came around, he would call all the poor and needy to come and fill their cars or carts with food. This commandment was according to Leviticus 19: 9, 10. This was most beneficial for the people, as this was the time of the Great Depression. My father often told us of how happy this would make our grandfather to see the people ate to their fill, especially the children.

My grandfather also practiced the resting of his land every seventh year. Yet no one quite understood the significance of his actions, thinking of him only to be a good man. I can still hear the prayers that resounded in the evenings as he called out to his God for his blessings upon his children. I remember the wonderful meals that my grandmother made for us on Sabbath; she always required all her children and their children to be present. Every meal began with the washing of hands, the breaking of the bread and the prayer of thanksgiving. She never left the house without her head covered and never allowed her hair to be cut. I can still see my mother combing her long locks that almost reached below her knees.

My great Uncle Marcos (Mark) taught me, my brothers and sisters to make Spanish cookies called *biscoches* also known as *biscochitos*. It turns out that they really were called Haman's cap and celebrated Queen Esther's efforts to save her people.

I have had the opportunity to sit with many Anusim and have listened to their tragic stories. Many have suffered at the hands of the Mexican immigration services. They have been beaten, starved, and mistreated so badly (not even an animal should be treated so grievously). No word of their whereabouts is ever given to their friends or family. The forces of evil have attacked some of our people with powerful spirits of depression and addictions to all sorts of drugs and alcohol. Poverty has sunk its teeth into our youth, and they have tragically turned to crime as a means for survival. Clearly, the purpose of these attacks is to destroy Gods children before they have a chance to hear of the story of who we really are and the redemptive role we have in life. However, Adonai has promised to give us the victory. We the Anusim must rise up as a people and shake off these evil attacks and possess the land that has been promised to us. When we do this, we will see the fulfillment of Zachariah's words in chapter 13 verse 10, *…And I will pour upon the house of David and upon the inhabitance of Jerusalem the spirit of Grace and supplication…* Our prayers to HaShem will give us the grace to overcome any obstacle that the enemy may place in our road to victory. We will fulfill our destiny in prophecy.

Cari Gillespie's Story
New Mexico, USA

Cari Gillespi (right) and Daughter

I had always known that I am Hispanic, but the Jewish part of this story was a secret. Strangely enough, I had spent my entire life deeply troubled by the inner knowledge that something about my personal identity was being kept from me. As I grew older, this deeply troubled me. As a child, I was certain that my parents were not my biological parents. I kept asking my sisters for information and was always ridiculed. In my mid-forties, this was nearly to the point of destroying my life. I prayed fervently that my God would reveal to me who I really am.

About eighteen years ago, I traveled to my home in Albuquerque, New Mexico to visit my parents and family. I was house-sitting for my younger sister while they were away on vacation in Europe. On the very last day that I was in town, I went to my parent's home for a last visit. When I got there, my mother told me that she needed to share something with me. It was obvious to me that she and Dad had been discussing this prior to my arrival, because Dad was silent and kept facing away from me.

Mother disappeared down the hallway and reappeared with a large, full page article from the *Albuquerque Journal* that was published during the Easter season a few months earlier. The article was about the Hispanic Jews of New Mexico and the research being done by the History Department of the University of New Mexico. She told me that she had been keeping this article for my arrival, as she didn't want to share the information over the phone. As I sat on the sofa and read the article, with both parents being strangely silent, my mother told me that she had a secret for me. She asked me if I remembered the family reunion for the Elorreaga family in El Paso, Texas many years previously. I had not been able to attend that reunion, but all of my sisters and cousins did. So did my parents. I was the only one not in attendance.

Almost out of nowhere, Mom said, "You are a Jew!" I was stunned. She told me that on that occasion of the family reunion, uncle Max, from Mexico City, came forward to share what he felt was a "shameful secret." He was quite old and could not go to his grave without telling all the family this "shameful secret." He gave all the information of our Hebrew history.

Adding to this, my family had advertised the reunion in all the major newspapers of the Southwest, California, Texas and Mexico. Most of the family is still in Mexico. Because of this advertising, a history professor from the University of Mexico, in Mexico City, asked if he might speak. He told us that our family was his hobby. He had thoroughly researched the Elorreaga family and gave much history of the family and confirmed our Hebrew roots.

This reunion had taken place at least ten years earlier so I asked Mom why she had never told me a thing about this before. She gave some stupid excuse about shame, but the truth is that she had lived her entire life being extremely anti-Semitic. Dad had also. Now, they had to admit the shameful secret.

When I had the opportunity to visit with my three sisters and all my cousins, they admitted that they had heard the stories and believed them. However, they were either hard core Catholic and didn't want to change, or they were ashamed and wanted it to remain a secret. I must admit that for almost two decades I was the only person in the family to accept my identity and do something about it. However, I received much persecution from my sisters, parents, cousins, and family friends. I held my stand and can now say that my younger sister wants more information and the other remaining sister is interested.

Shortly after this revelation, my mother had some strange reason to be in contact with a cousin from the other side of her family. He had done an extensive history and genealogy of the Garcia family and proved that this branch of the family is also Hebrew. From there, my son and his wife have taken that information and carried it much farther into the European histories all the way back prior to the Inquisition which was a horrendous holocaust in Spain and also Portugal and later Mexico.

If anyone had asked me earlier what I felt my reaction might be if I had been told that I was a Jewish woman, I have no idea what I would have done. When I finally found out, I felt that God hovered over me in a very special way. I was so excited that I could scarcely get out of my parent's home fast enough. I made quick excuses about packing my bags and sleeping well for the flight home the next day. I went to bed in my sister's room that had a wonderful mountain view of the city of Albuquerque, which is quite beautiful in the night lights. I didn't sleep much. I watched the city lights all night as I felt God's Spirit intimately dealing with me. He showed me that my hidden identity which was withheld from me and had nearly ruined my life was now complete. I finally knew who I am.

It is not possible to put the experiences of that night in the presence of God dealing with my innermost feelings in a most intimate way. This joy wasn't simply because I finally know who I truly am. I was joyful at knowing that I am a Hebrew. Imagine that! I never would have expected to feel that way.

Since that time, I have deeply held my Jewishness and have been an avid learner of all that is available to me. I am most interested not only in the Hebrew language and the original scripts in Hebrew, but the root meanings of those words and how profoundly they affect the understanding of Holy Scriptures which is in opposition to the man-made doctrines of the Christian Church. This is a fascinating life, being a Hebrew—being a Jew.

Although I have kept my story short, there are volumes of blessings as well as solid knowledge in connection with this. I never dreamed that knowing God would be so deep, so rich and so powerful in my daily life. I never knew that I would amass new knowledge which I have researched together with the findings of my children. I feel sorry for so many people that are still stuck in anti-Semitic congregations with limited knowledge and distorted information. The good news is that more and more people like me are coming out of the catacombs of ignorance and beginning to move towards the light of their true heritage and their destiny.

My advice to whoever reads this story is to begin asking questions and demanding answers that are consistent with truth and our blood that's crying out.

Tatiana Barrera Guzmán's Story
Northern Mexico

Tatiana Barrera Guzman

The way I discovered that I am a Sephardic Jew did not arrive over night. It was a process in my life that started from my childhood.

When I was seven years old or younger, my mother started to teach me the stories of the bible where God stands with his people–the people of Israel. She told me the stories of the Tanakh (Old Testament) such as Noah, Samson, Jonah, David, Joseph, Moses and many more. All those stories stayed very fresh in my heart. At that time, I never thought I was part of those stories, but in the bottom of my heart I yearned to be without knowing that I really was.

Around that same time, my best friend, with whom my sister and I spent almost every afternoon playing, was a Jewish boy. His mother and mine were good friends and shared many activities together, especially recipes. I have a very clear memory when I saw my friend dressed very formally and with his yarmulke or kippa on Saturday morning and asked him where he was going. He told me he was going to their local synagogue together with his family.

I remember insistently asking to take me with his family that I wanted to go to synagogue too. But obviously, my mother did not give me permission and she said to me that we were going to Catholic Church the next day. But in my heart I preferred going with my friend and his family because something deep within me drew me in that direction.

Some years later, my family decided to move north into the countryside near my mom's family. That was how we eventually moved to Saltillo, Coahuila, Mexico. It was here that I continued learning about God and having a closer relationship with Him. I must say that during all this time I yearned to know if, per chance, I had any Jewish blood in my veins. I do not know why I had this profound longing; I just know that I occasionally sighed and asked God, "Why am I not a Jew?" The truth is that I always knew that being Jewish was not required to approach God nor to worship Him and for Him to listen to me. I do not know how to explain why the desire was so overwhelming in my heart to belong to the Jewish community. My mom always taught us too love Israel more than any other country or people.

As a child, I remember my family used to have certain habits that none of my friends used to have at home. For example, we were forbidden to eat pork regardless of how it was cooked or who was serving it. I never asked why, simply because as a child I was instructed not to do certain kinds of things. This was the standard of our family.

My grandmother used to light candles on Friday night. One day, her children asked her why she did that and she confessed that she did not know. She simply stated, "Just because my mother used to do it also."

The harder process began when I was in a period of life when I no longer knew what course to follow. I was wandering aimlessly. One day I went to a local bookstore to find a gift for my dad whose birthday was the following day. The truth is that I saw many titles of good books but none that I knew my father would like. So I decided to ask the bookstore manager if he could recommend me a good book to give as a present to a mature man. He looked at me and after thinking a little bit he showed me a book entitled *Hebrew Roots*. I looked at him and I made a gesture of dissent after all, my Dad has never been very religious so the title won't even look interesting to him. He stared at me and refuted saying, "Do you know that you're probably Jewish?"

This question left me cold and unresponsive, so he continued by saying, "Tell me what your last name is and perhaps your last name is on the list in this book."

I remember superficially saying, "I do not think my last name is Jewish, my father's family comes from Spain not Israel." He began to search the list that came at the end of the book and surprisingly found it. My eyes instantly filled with uncontrollable tears and he explained to me the story of how many Spanish Jews had been forced to leave Spain by the Inquisition. Without thinking anymore, I purchased the book. Instantly, I began to read with eagerness and it relit the flame that had been in my heart since I was a child.

This book began to give me much needed direction for my life. From that moment, I started looking for more information, with the help and support of my husband, who also has a story about this matter. I searched my roots on both my father and my mother's sides. I began to find more information on my mother's side regarding their Sephardic Jewishness.

Now I had some information and a belief on where my roots were from, but where to from here? It was when my husband and I attended a special conference which explained who the Sephardic Anusim Jews are and we began to see much clearer what our purpose is in life. We learned much about our roots and the need for us to return to our forefathers' homeland in order to accomplish God's promises. Specially, we learned about our prophesied destiny to occupy the Negev of Israel and to collaborate in preparing the way for Messiah's coming.

Now everything is clearer, though not easy, but we are in this process God has called us to follow. Day by day, little by little, we see how everything is taking shape. This is why my husband, our son and I travel over six hours, one way, from our city in northern Mexico to be at the synagogue of our choosing in San Antonio, Texas. Yes it is tough but we would have it no other way. We are learning much there and have been warmly embraced and helped by the rabbis and the Jewish fellowship. We even participate in a special Jewish class taught by a Jewish leader in our synagogue delivered to us over the internet via Skype all the way from San Antonio, Texas to Saltillo, Mexico.

When we traveled to Israel on a pilot visit which is mandatory before immigrating to Israel, we experienced nothing but affirmation and renewed conviction that we are on the right track. Therefore, our plans are to make Aliyah and become Israeli citizens as soon as God releases us to do so.

I wish to say that we are not the only ones in Saltillo, Mexico or this region of our Republic that have Sephardic roots. After all, the actual founders of our country and particularly our city were Sephardic explorers and Conquistadors such as Del Canto and Montemayor. They settled our land together with a host of precious Sephardic families just like us.

Jesse Gonzalez' Story
Texas, USA

Jesse Gonzalez

My name is Jesse Gonzalez. I am from the barrios (neighborhoods) of San Antonio, Texas. My story began when I met my wife, Lisa in 1990. She noticed that some of my siblings spelled our last name with an "s" and others with a "z" at the end. I used to spell my name with an "s." I did not realize this until she brought it to my attention. So she went to the Health Department to get a copy of my birth certificate. Lo and behold it was spelled with a "z." In time, this would become a turning point in my life. All this time I had been spelling my last name with an "s." I also saw on the certificate my father's name was spelled with a "z" as well. Needless to say all documents were changed accordingly. I do not know why I felt that this was so important to me. Was it because an error was corrected or the truth was revealed? I later learned that "ez" as well as "es" meant son of the Land of Israel, as in "Erez (or Eres) Israel."

When I was a child, I remember seeing my grandmother do certain peculiar things one of which was lighting two candles each Friday night. Now I know that this was the beginning of the Sabbath also known as Shabbat. I can remember her making a fuss about the most delicious bread called, *Pan de Semita* (bread with anise seeds and without leaven which actually means bread of Semites or Jews). This bread always had a very special smell and taste, different to all others. Everyone loved it. I now realize that was our own "Challa bread" which is customarily eaten on Shabbat.

Each year during Passover, grandmother would make a bread pudding called, *Capirotada* which is a mixture of cooked bread, cheese, raisins, peanuts, and crystallized sugarcane juice. This is so similar to the Jewish "Charoset."

I remember seeing my *tias* (aunts) dip their fingers in the holy water dispenser as they entered our home. Then they made the sign of the cross on their forehead, chest, left shoulder, right shoulder, and then kissed their thumb. I later found out a Jewish mezuzah was behind the water dispenser. Many other gestures were performed that were very different to most other families in our *barrio*. At that time and for most of my life, I had no idea what I was headed for. It never entered my mind that we may be Jewish. This was just our way of life in our little west side *barrio*.

One day we heard there was going to be a conference on Spanish Jews. Curiosity pulled us to listen. At first we were a little skeptical and felt we might be wasting our time. We heard about the Spanish and Mexican Inquisitions and how our forefathers were victims in those holocausts. Slowly it began to sink in, "Hey could it be that we're the children of these dear victims?"

Then it came to the part of the torturing because some Jews would not convert to Catholicism; and others did for survival purposes but only after terrific coercion. I discovered that many Sephardic Jews were Catholics by day but Jews by night. So a small light bulb went off in my head and I wondered, "Could it be? No, it can't be. But how could it be? Is it possible?" I began to get very emotional and started weeping because of the prospect that I was actually a descendant of Sephardic Jews that had gone underground in order to survive. I had mixed emotions. Then I got very angry because I had been lied to and I was upset because my ancestors went through all this torture and suffering for so many generations and my family and I didn't know a thing about it.

All the pieces of the puzzle were finally coming together. But the icing on the cake was when my DNA results came back and showed me that I was of the J1 haplotype on my father's side. This confirms that I am a Jew and it could be that I am from the line of Levi, but further testing is required in order to find this out for sure. There is even a probability that my continued DNA test analysis will reveal that I may be of the Cohanim line which is a direct descendant of the line of Israel's first High Priest who was Moses' brother, specifically Aaron. Whether I'm a Cohen or not is not the point. The point is that hard science proves that I come from a very long Biblical line of Jews who dwelled in Israel as far back as 4000 years ago.

Wow! Now I know who I am and where I need to go. My work has just begun. I will be telling my siblings of my research and that they too are descendants of hidden Sephardic Jews. Hopefully we will all make aliyah some day and become full blown Israeli citizens–specifically living in the Negev. But "Why the Negev?" you ask. The Negev because the ancient Bible prophet named Obadiah foretold that the "Exiles of Jerusalem who are (were) in Sepharad (Spain) will return and occupy the Negev," (Obadiah verse 20). So I greatly look forward to this journey whatever the cost.

Javier Gonzales' Story
Colorado, USA

Javier Gonzales

The term "Anusim" is used to describe 15th Century Jews who were forced to convert to Christianity, who most likely lost their identity through assimilation into the Catholic faith. Anusim, also known as Crypto-Jews can be found in present day Portugal, Spain, the United States, Latin America and the Caribbean Islands. All indications point to the fact that both my maternal and paternal grandmothers, Franscisca Soto and Maria Salgado were descendents of these Iberian Jews. They were from a small town 60 miles southeast of Chihuahua City, Mexico.

As a small child and adolescent, I would travel with my parents to Chihuahua City, Delicias, and Julimes, Mexico to visit my grandparents and extended family during summer vacations and the holidays (Christmas). On Fridays both my grandmothers would light two candles and since I was raised as a Catholic, I didn't give it much thought. I am unsure if they were aware of their Anusim background and it is very probable that their identity was lost as I believe that they were part of a large group of Jews known as *Nuevos Cristianos* (New Christians) or *conversos* who came across the ocean and settled in the New World.

In the small community where they lived there were around eight to ten families that would celebrate the traditional Christian holiday of Christmas and they would also observe it by placing eight candles inside small brown paper bags filled with sand. I remember playing with the children in that community using a *trompo* that had four sides with markings on it. Later in life, I found that this *trompo* was of European origin; the European Jews call it a dreidel and use it during Chanukah.

My family in Mexico also abstained from leavened bread during *La Semana Santa* or *La Semana Mayor* (The Holy Week or The Major Week). During this time, I enjoyed eating a sweet dish; this food was made with unleavened bread and called *capirotada*. On many occasions while staying with my paternal grandmother, I saw her praying and reciting Psalm 23. She told me many times to memorize the psalm and she was very emphatic about it. A Rabbi friend of mine told me that Jews of Belmonte, Portugal would memorize this particular Psalm to help them deal with the hardships of the Inquisition. While I believe it's unlikely that my grandmother was from Portugal because my uncles and aunts told me that my great grandmother was from Spain; nevertheless, I'm certain that many Sephardic Anusim had relatives in both, Spain as well as Portugal. I have since memorized Psalm 23 in Hebrew.

In his book, "Secrecy and Deceit: The religion of the Crypto-Jews," Dan Gitlitz documents customs practiced by the Sephardic Jews in pre-expulsion Spain. While growing up I observed some of these practices in my family, such as slaughtering poultry and livestock by cutting the throat and completely draining the blood. I did not observe Jewish lifecycle events such as Brit Milah or Bar/Bat Mitzvah. This is probably due to the fact that after conversion the inquisitors would still check for Jewish practices. With the passing of time many *conversos* never returned to the custom of lifecycle events.

I am aware that it's been said that many conversos became more observant Catholics than the majority of Catholics. This was done to avoid detection and eventual persecution. My uncle told me that my maternal Grandfather, Jose de la Luz Segovia would oftentimes stand outside the Catholic Church and curse the priest and that he was not as observant as my grandmother. Several times I heard them talking about *Los Sefarditas* but I didn't understand the meaning and it didn't interest me. However, an aunt of mine once told me that she was constantly told by her father about the tragedies that befell the Jewish people during Tisha B'Av and specifying the expulsion of the Jews from Spain on Tisha B'Av. (This day is also known as the 9th of Av and is connected to phenomenal tragedies that have fallen on Israel and Jews around the world on that infamous day.)

It was not until I enlisted in the Army in 1991 that during basic training I started to suspect and inquire about my Jewishness. A friend of mine who happened to be Jewish told me in a matter of fact way that I was Jewish just like him and I recently found that the Patronic Crest of Soto has the Star of David on it. Soto so happens to also be my maternal grandmother's family name.

On my first trip to Erez Israel I researched the archives of Holocaust names on the database at the Yad Vashem Memorial and was amazed to find that there were many Soto Jews from Salonika, Greece that perished during World War II. I was not raised as a Jew or in Judaism but many of the memories I have described and the documented history of the Anusim have made me aware that I am. This knowledge has given me a desire to find out more about my Jewish roots.

While I have never directly experienced anti-Semitism but I'll relate a curious story that happened to me a few years ago. While serving in the Army, one of my female commanders disliked me for no particular reason so she went out of her way to accuse me of many things I didn't do. She would use foul language to belittle me in front of my peers. She was a German who immigrated to the United States. I've often wondered if her German world view has had any influence in her behavior seeing that I am of a Jewish Anusim heritage. I tend to believe her attitude against my Jewishness is intentional but neither is it coincidental.

The Prophet Jeremiah describes a time when His people will live in safety and acknowledge the Almighty and His Messiah: "The days are coming," declares the LORD, "when I will raise up to David a righteous Branch, a King who will reign wisely and do what is just and right in the land. In his days Judah will be saved and Israel will live in safety. This is the name by which he will be called: The LORD Our Righteousness."

Knowing this promise about dwelling safely in the Land and being made righteous through our coming Messiah has given me profound hope and a will to some day make Aliyah and to live as an Israeli citizen; so I am now actively planning our Aliyah so that my family and I may return to the Land of Abraham Avinu.

Arlene Iacone's Story
Florida, USA

Arlene Iacone

The name given to me at birth was Arlene Ayala Cuevas (Ayala for my Dad and Cuevas for my Mom), that is the Spanish way.

God gave me a vision on August 1, 2005 which changed our lives forever. The vision has to do with our rapid and urgent departure from the United States to Israel. In fact, I actually met a central figure in this vision during a recent Sephardic Anusim conference in the Negev of Israel.

A year later, while watching television, a gentleman said something that touched my soul very profoundly because it further legitimized the vision I had the previous year.

The man on TV said something to this effect: *You Spanish p[eople] love the Jewish people and their land very much. Many of you attend synagogues or congregations along with them. Many of your names end with the letters e-s or e-z. Some of you have received heavenly revelations. I am here to tell you that you are of a Jewish ancestry.*

I have no words to describe what took place in my soul as I heard a person that's not even of my own heritage pronounce these words. His words more than legitimized my profound feelings towards my Jewish family and Erez Israel.

All the pieces of the puzzle in my vision suddenly fell into place. I can say that I could almost hear God chuckle at my childlike joy. The guests on this television program confirmed to me who I really am. It was as if I had finally found my true self by the verification of someone else. This has changed my life. I have started on a wonderful journey. Now I wish to share a few of the stories we held tightly and secretly to.

I remember my eldest sister telling me that our great grandmother about five generations ago, of the Medina family, was known to be a Jew in faith along with her entire family. She was not given any other information because it was a family secret. This was on my father's side.

On my mother's side we discovered that a lot of the breads my grandfather baked were, in fact, Jewish. He was a great baker who also taught my mother who in turn taught me the art of Jewish baking. Today I am teaching my daughter, Jessica. One of my favorite breads grandfather baked was called *pan de huevo* which means bread made with eggs. This was in Lares, Puerto Rico. As it turns out, this was our Jewish Challah bread.

My mother told me that as children around the first of fall, grandfather would make each of his nine children bread for each of them in the form of a dove. He was also known for his *pan de budin* which is what's called, kruggle. In the spring this bread was made without yeast.

Dell F. Sanchez, Ph.D.

Her mother died when she was a young teen. I was told she could embroider very beautifully. My mother was also very good at this ancient Sephardic artwork. In fact, mother knew how to create what's called the *mondillo*, a lost art of making lace handed down from one generation to another. Her *mondillo* sets are now in a Museum in Moca, Puerto Rico which is my father's hometown.

As a family we are on a Journey to make Aliyah as soon as we can. We have gone on our aliyah pilot trip to Israel with a group of fellow Sephardic Anusim. Besides loving our tour through much of Israel, we were honored to be at a Sephardic Anusim Conference for three days in the land our people are to inherit, the Negev.

Presently, as a family, we're taking Hebrew lessons as we learn to read and write Hebrew. We also attend Shabbat services and other holy day events in our local synagogue. We also volunteer to assist with different Jewish functions including teaching on Sephardic Anusim history. We are doing everything possible to be "good Jews." I say this because this has come after 500 years since our Sephardic ancestors went underground and have lived a life of secrecy and hiding. But now we're coming out of our closets and fulfilling our destiny.

Joseph S. Berrios-Zaborsky's Story
Florida, USA

Joseph S. Berrios

The discovery of my Jewish ancestry has been a journey of joy and at the same time of grief and sadness. My journey started when I decided to pursue theological studies. My desire to pursue these studies was to acquire tools to help me develop a closer relationship with God. Originally I started the Masters of Divinity at a local seminary under the sponsorship of a Protestant denomination. By the way, I also hold a Ph.D. degree.

While pursuing these studies a series of intriguing events led me to discover that I had a Jewish ancestry. As a Latino, I carry both my mother and father's last name. My case is not unlike many other Latinos in my country. I say this because my mother is a descendant of Ashkenazi Jews from Hungary. Her maiden name is Zaborsky which is a Jewish last name, unlike my father's Latino last name and upbringing.

My father is a descendant of *conversos* (Sephardic Jews that were forced to convert to Catholicism during the Spanish Inquisition). This fact was confirmed through DNA test analysis that I carry the Jewish genetic code. This discovery has sparked a deep yearning in my soul to reclaim my Jewish heritage.

Meantime, the pastor of the church I used to attend proclaimed behind the pulpit that he was pro-Israel and that he had Jewish blood. However, since my slow conversion back to Judaism, this pastor has made my life literally miserable. One day, while counseling me in his office he suddenly told me that he was a Gentile and that I should not 'go back' to Judaism because I was going to lose the "salvation by grace." Then he started to talk about a "two covenant theology."

His theology is based on the assumption that Gentiles are saved through grace by merely believing in the Messiah of Israel. On the other hand, Jews are saved by how well they keep the Law also known as the Torah. Unfortunately it is taught in some Gentile Christian circles that the biggest difference between the ways of the God of the Tanakh, and the ways of the New Testament God is that a believer has to work to attain his righteousness in the Tanakh, and the Christian receives it as a gift. In addition, this teaching includes that good works lead a man to some *undefined kind of salvation* in the Tanakh, and grace through faith brings a man to *a well-defined kind of salvation* in what Christians call "The New Covenant."

My opinion is that if you read the works (commentaries) of the ancient sages, or later, the Rabbis, you will find a great emphasis placed on doing God's commands, which Christians usually call "works" and "legalism." However, the actual reason for Israel's motivation with good

deeds and an active faith system is less a matter of gaining some
from it than from obedience due to the overwhelming gratefulness to
being a member of the community of God's Chosen People.

All this brings me to one of the issues that breaks my heart. I'm referring to the rejection that my people, the Sephardic Anusim Jews, often get from Jews that are generally of an Ashkenazi heritage. (I must include the fact that on the other hand, I've also experienced much rejection from Christian circles which only complicates things in my life.) I consider myself blessed in the sense that my mother has an Ashkenazi heritage, but generally Sephardic Jews from Latin America have a real hard time proving their Jewish ancestry.

Unfortunately during the Spanish inquisition, almost all records of Jewish ancestry were destroyed. The goal of the Spanish crown was to eradicate all traces of Jewish linage and by these actions they robbed us from the integrity of our soul and also our cultural identity.

I have witnessed that when Hispanics discover their Sephardic Anusim ancestry they are treated as a *wanna-be* Jew by most other Jews. As stated earlier, I've also discovered that many Christians act suspiciously, with an attitude of alienation and rejection. At best, many Christians make full attempts to convince us that they're right and we're wrong.

I am persuaded that Jews as well as Christians who down-right reject Sephardic Anusim do not realize that by their actions they are fulfilling the desires of Spain's Inquisition masters, Queen Isabella and King Ferdinand. They do not appear to know that they are serving to eradicate the Jewish ancestry from Sephardic Anusim who has a long Jewish bloodline.

In this era when all Jews are facing challenges which threaten our existence, we need to come together as one nation—one people. We need to reach out to the Sephardic Anusim and to help them reclaim their lost heritage as sons of Abraham, Isaac and Jacob. And we need to be patient with them as they endure the long journey of unlearning and disconnecting from so much Greco-Roman (Christian) theology which is saturated with many forms of paganism all across the board. And we need to gently and circumspectly help them as they reconnect to their ancient Jewish family in ways that'll bless everyone, including Erez Israel.

Leticia Soto
Northern Mexico/South Texas

Leticia Soto

My name is Leticia Soto and I was born to parents whose descendents are from Northern Mexico and Southern Texas. The Sephardic Jewish legacy in Northern México, especially in the area of Nuevo León, was not unknown to me, but I never imagined I had a connection to the Jews who settled there centuries ago.

In July 2009, my love for international cooking and personal interest in Judaism led to discover our Sephardic heritage through my matrilineal line. While reading a Jewish cookbook, I came across a

Sephardic recipe similar to one of my mother's. After some probing, she revealed indications of Jewish traditions that were practiced by elder family members.

My mother's great grand-parents, Eulalia Benavides de Lozano and Rafael Lozano de la Garza, were from Los Herreras, Nuevo León, México. "Mamá Lalita" as Eulalia was called, had taught all the females specific recipes which in turn were taught to my mother. "Mamá Lalita" was known to be adamant about keeping the Sabbath because God commanded it. Her Friday mornings were spent making bread, pastries, and other foods in preparation for the family's evening meal.

On Saturday, they would eat leftovers heated on a metal griddle and do nothing else throughout the day as work was not permitted. On Sunday, she would resume her chores. She frequently stated that the week was supposed to start on Sunday and disapproved of Monday having become the commonly accepted start of the week. As a child, my mother would hear Mamá Lalita privately say to her daughters and grand-daughters that to say that one was a Jew was a death sentence and it was better to keep one's mouth shut. She would say Jews always suffered because the word "Jew" equaled persecution. The Holocaust occurred during my mother's childhood and I imagine this could have had some bearing on these secret conversations. My mother would be shooed away, but would over hear.

Rafael Lozano de la Garza, my great great-grandfather, was a successful butcher who raised cattle, goats and sheep. When he took his animals to the slaughterhouse, they were killed by having their throats slit and its blood thoroughly drained.

My grandmother, Manuela Lozano de Rodriguez, (Eulalia and Rafael's granddaughter), would tell her children that the world would be a better place when the Messiah appears. She would also speak about the suffering encountered by the Jewish people and how at times Jews would withhold their identity from one another to avoid being betrayed or exposed. These betrayals are exactly what occurred during the Inquisition and centuries later, amazingly, my grandmother relayed this to her children during family conversations.

The experience of the Sephardic Jews is not a common topic among most people. Yet, its vestiges were remembered and discussed among the elder women of my mother's family. I presume they were transmitted through preceding generations of relatives who had escaped the Inquisition. They are valued and precious references to my family history and its connection to Jewish traditions.

Discovering this facet of my identity has been surprising and exciting, but at times presents internal challenges to the spiritual concepts and practices I was raised with as they were not Jewish. Nonetheless, I've openheartedly embraced my Jewish heritage with all its inherent beauty and tribulations. The study of the Torah is an important part of my life, leading me to a deeper understanding of HaShem and His will for humanity. Inevitably, this has also caused a greater appreciation for Israel and raised the question of making aliyah. To this I say, if it is part of my destiny to live in Israel, then so be it.

Francisco Javier Lizarraga Lopez
Northern Mexico

Francisco Javier Lizarraga Lopez

It all began in the state of Sonora, Mexico which borders the State of Arizona, USA. When I was child my mother taught me to love and revere God above all things. From an early age I had a zeal for the things of God. I've always had feelings which are almost impossible to explain. I heard stories about Old Testament characters such as Noah, Moses, Joseph, David and many more. I was fascinated with the manner in which God took His Chosen People, the Israelites, out of bondage. I often asked my mother why I wasn't Jewish and she would only smile and hug me.

My youth was devoted to studies and family. However I always felt a profound feeling in my heart that I was, somehow, part of Israel but couldn't understand it. Within was a fire to know all I could about God which lasted through my youth. God managed to always show me that he was with me.

During my college days, I met a beautiful girl who in the future became my wife. She loved dancing and most of all, Hebrew dances. Together we started to talk about Israel and we realized we both had the same concern since our childhood and we both agreed with deep consternation why we weren't born a Jew.

One day my wife arrived home very happy explaining to me that we could be Jewish because she had read a book which states that many early settlers of northern Mexico were Jewish. They had been forced to change their religion by the incredible pressures of the Spanish as well as the Mexican Inquisitions. In fact, we discovered that the Inquisitors used all types of torture ranging from mental to psychological as well as physical torture. The book included a list of Spanish Jewish surnames. My heart must have contracted as I slowly began to seek my last name in that list. To my shock, my name appeared in that list. I couldn't believe it. After many years, my childhood yearnings began to reveal a truth which could not remain hidden any longer.

I have since discovered that my own ancestors were Sephardic Jews who were forced to change their Jewish faith and customs and to adopt a Roman Catholic religion. They were forced to betray their own heritage and identity in order to avoid the Inquisition's wrath which included public humiliations as well as burnings at the stake all because they were Jews. We have been on an investigative journey ever since the day we discovered our names in that book.

Not long afterwards, as if heaven's fate had dictated, we attended a conference on the history of Sephardic Anusim Jews here in Mexico and our eyes were opened even more widely. I took my investigation to another level of interviewing my older family members in search for facts or the slightest clues that could lead me to the next dimension of our quest. Some of our questions had to do with our grandparents and their parents and their parent's parents. The more we inquired the more we unearthed little secrets that pointed to the reality that we were on the right path and that we were to never abandon our journey nor ever allow anyone to influence the betrayal of our true roots and heritage.

After some time, my mother finally confessed that my grandfather was always called a Jew in his town. Unfortunately I never met my grandfather and my mother was departed from him since she was child. From that moment I met my true identity–I finally discovered my history as well as my destiny. Now I fight with great passion to awaken and to educate my son to return and recover our identity as a Jewish family. Together, my wife and our son have found a purpose and a mission which will eventually lead us back to the home of our forefathers in Israel, and particularly "our Negev."

Possibly the single most significant thing that has happened to us in our journey is that, every weekend, we take a six hour trip to be at our synagogue where we are treated with dignity and respect. Every Friday afternoon, as soon as my wife and I get out from work, we take this long haul across the U.S.-Mexican border in order to be at our wonderful Shabbat (Sabbath) services on Saturday morning. We are always happy to see our Jewish friends and to fellowship with them during Kiddush and other meals. I feel proud that some of the men of stature have invited me to sit in the front row in synagogue during services.

There are times the border is extremely busy and also very guarded due to narco-traffic and recent warfare between narcotic overlords and local and federal police forces. But none of this stops us from doing what's deep in our hearts because we have finally found our real family and they treat us as members as well. So it is that every Friday we head north and then on Sunday we head south, back home to be ready for work on Monday–always looking forward to our time with our Jewish family as we're being groomed to some day be in the home of our real destiny which is the Negev of Israel.

Chapter Seven – Synthesis of Personal Evidences

The Oral Histories

Each oral history in the section above has demonstrated personal and intimate information. They have revealed family secrets and referred to the life cycle as related to their Sephardic journey. These contributors have shared issues of their soul–something that Sephardic Crypto-Jews do not often do with "outsiders."

We have seen the general mosaic of these Sephardic Anusim. They have told us of their feasts but also their fears. They have shared secrets that had been held, as it were, in the airtight chambers of their memory up until today.

They have opened their heart to give us their paternal and maternal surnames most of which are Sephardic in origin. They have also shared with us some of the foods that were quite kosher, as well as a few of the sayings known as *dichos y refranes*. We have discovered that in many instances, with or without their knowing, they married *entre la misma gente*–among their same people. In other words, we find Sephardic men marrying Sephardic women and stressing upon their children to marry among their own people in order to perpetuate a Sephardic presence and lifestyle.

We have heard the stories of men and women sharing what and how they learned of their hidden Sephardic secrets. In some instances we discovered amazing genealogies that point all the way back to the 1500s which are connected to great Sephardic Conquistadors such as Don Luis de Carvajal, Don Juan de Oñate, de Vargas, del Canto and Montemayor. On the other hand, we also discovered a number of cases where their DNA has been scientifically proven to be of Sephardic origins. One of them happens to be a Cohen–a direct descendant of Aaron, the first High Priest of Israel and Moses' elder brother.

What stands out the most is the emotional impact these contributors experienced when they discovered or confirmed their Sephardic ancestry. Personally, I am quite impressed with the deep sense of dignity and self-worth which has come as a direct result due to their discovering the truth of their ancestry. At last, they found their true forefathers and have been embraced by a new spirit of belonging.

I happen to know the majority of these contributors on a personal basis. I have not only heard elements of their stories that are way more profound than this record reveals; but I have also witnessed the stirring in their heart as they discovered and confirmed the truth of their heritage. I have seen the joy and the tears that have spoken much louder than their abbreviated histories. For the most part, they have been in hiding while their families held their secrets close to their heart. I am also impressed by the fact that, all along, they have continued to allow those that mislabeled them think they agreed with such erroneous stereotypes.

So it is that we have gone full circle as we moved from the documented historical record and on through material evidences, onomastics and DNA. It is most becoming that we have ended not with more data and information, but with living parables.

There is something very sacred to the stories these oral historians have shared with us. I believe the time has come to set the record straight, to start teachings this knowledge in our homes and in our schools. It is time to educate our national and our religious leaders regarding this knowledge. And it is time to do whatever it takes to exonerate and to commend these Sephardic Anusim for their perseverance and willingness to come out of hiding. The collective story of these people must never again be forgotten.

Chapter Eight – Implications and Projections

This section raises the question, "Where to from here?" A decision needs to be made whether this book will have served for the benefit of "pure knowledge" or if it will also prompt the reader to some form of action. In any case, what kind of impact might the awakening of Sephardic Anusim create in society? What kind of things might take place as the awakening of Sephardic Anusim continues to grow into exponentially figures? What impact might this phenomenon create in churches, synagogues and particularly in the halls of Israeli agencies as they clamor to be accepted as a Israeli citizens?

Based on the developments of the last ten to fifteen years, I foresee a massive emergence of hidden Sephardic Anusim that will get our nation's attention. I believe we are on the verge of seeing a number of key governmental leaders respond to the outcry among those longing to get reconnected to their true and authentic roots and to return to the land of their forefathers, Israel.

Meantime, I foresee an exodus of Sephardic Anusim from irrelevant Christian churches that can not or will not relate to their peculiar needs. Some of them will become dynamically involved in local synagogues. Some Jewish rabbis and leaders will arise to lend them a hand. I also foresee an underground movement of worship and Torah studies with a prophetic orientation based on ancient Bible prophecies. These will be among those that stand in the gap to advocate on behalf of Sephardic Anusim before agencies and institutions that hold power to make a positive difference in their lives.

Seeing how the Sephardic Anusim community is scattered across tens of thousands of square miles all across the Americas from Canada to the United States and down to Mexico, Central and South America, new avenues of communication and relationship will emerge. While there shall be various camps of Sephardic Anusim representing the diverse expressions of their faith and ancestry, a central and unifying camp will arise to serve as a trusted mediator between the diverse camps and schools of thought. Many of them will see the urgency to set their differences aside, to unite and work together to achieve a common cause. They will recognize that it has forever been the will of their perpetrators to keep them divided; so with fervor they will arise above those ancient partitions that held so many apart, not only from each other but also from their common family, the Jewish community.

Many Sephardic Anusim will pressure Israeli law makers and institutions with authority over Aliyah (immigration) to reassess the Law of Return and to make special provisions for them to be received as citizens. One of the things that will prod this matter will be the emergence of wealthy Americans and other international leaders that will catch the vision to help them spiritually and financially in order to help them achieve their goals in the Negev and the whole of Israel.

In their new found zeal, these helps shall begin to invest into major projects in the Negev with dollars ear-marked for the building of homes, jobs and learning centers for Sephardic Anusim. These new and exciting developments in the Negev will attract untold numbers of tourists from around the world to visit Israel in order to see and experience this phenomenon. Like never before, tourists and serious seekers from Spanish speaking nations will be part of this entourage of onlookers that will take their message back home and thus create new waves of tourism, but of a different type.

On the other hand, as increased violence arises once again, with the prospects of war at an alarming rate, qualified Sephardic Anusim will be looked at through improved lenses in terms of citizenship. The powers-that-be will see that Sephardic Anusim families are large, young, energetic and very tenacious. This will be a desirable matter for the sake of Israel's future safety.

New methods of thinking and operating will be incorporated into old methods that have been in the Jewish community for many centuries. This will be seen in the light of a Moses-Joshua and an Elijah-Elisha era where the old embraces the young and together they move towards the enrichment of the Land and the people of Israel in preparation for the much anticipated coming of Messiah which most Jews yearn for.

Finally, something of utter importance will begin to shortly take place. The mysteries and undefined pathways for making Aliyah will alas come to the fore. The little nasty secrets that have been held for a long time by the subordinates of those in power over Aliyah will be exposed. Similar to the manner in which major American figures, institutions and corporations have been exposed, so will it be with those that have held an unjust and secretive reign over the Aliyah process. Major investigations will be commissioned as new legislation and legal enforcement will undergo a major overhaul. This process will most likely be prompted by chilling reports of injustice in high places alongside reports of a "Third Intifada" which will make the First and Second Intifadas pale.

Notwithstanding, Israel shall be delivered once again but not without the significant and much appreciated input from the Sephardic Anusim and their Zionists friends from around the world.

Conclusions

While in the office of the chairman of the board of the Jewish National Fund in Jerusalem, he declared to me that Israelis do not know who we are, referring to the American Anusim. They know a little of our history during the Spanish Inquisition and the manner in which our ancestors were labeled *Marranos*—meaning pigs. They know that most of the *Marranos* fled to many nations during attempts by the Spanish and Portuguese Inquisitions to annihilate them. However, he told me that they have no collective portrait of our people today and that we need to educate Israelis and Jews in general regarding who we are. This gentleman is so committed that he told our conference participants something I shall never forget. He said, "When I met Dell and Helen Sanchez and heard their story, I became a soldier of their cause." And he has proved it many times.

A few years later, during another Sephardic Anusim conference which we conducted in the Negev, a member of the Israeli Knesset emphatically told our group of American Anusim that we need to create a campaign to educate Israeli leaders as well as the grassroots of Israel about who we are. With earnest commitment he promised he would help us with this enormous task.

We, therefore, need to put a face to American Anusim. In this case, I am not referring to the Sephardic Anusim all across the Americas but only in the USA. Therefore, below is a profile that is a partial mosaic of the American Anusim today. My hope is to create such a portrait of all Sephardic Anusim in Diaspora.

I shall relate to the major variables, issues and concerns which make up this people group. They include elements of the physical, educational, occupational, familial, social values, socio-cultural characteristics, patriotism, Zionism and spiritual-religious issues.

Physical Characteristics

The Sephardic Anusim of America (referring only to the USA) are very much like today's Israeli society. I base this fact on almost 30 trips to Israel and in-depth interaction with Israeli leaders as well as the Israeli grassroots of society.

American Anusim are tall, short, stocky, lean, brown skin, dark hair and dark eyes as well as very light skin, blonde, reddish hair, blue and green eyes. Their diversity is enormous, just as it is in Israel. Some look very dark, almost black while others look very fair skin European.

Familial Characteristics

The American Anusim have larger families than all other races in America. The national average is 3.19 children per family–the Latino/Anusim family is 3.87 children per family. There is a huge difference in numbers when you set these figures into the millions. For instance, for every million families, there's a difference of approximately 680,000 more children within the Latino/Anusim home. At ten million families, the difference jumps to just under seven million more children.

It is a known fact that many Anusim families are larger in certain areas of the nation such as the Southwest. The median age of Latino/Anusim is 27.4, almost 10 years younger than the national norm. Two in every three homes have children under the age of 18.

Occupational and Educational Characteristics

The average income is close to $40,000 a year. They are considered to be a high consumer attraction to merchants at every level.

There is a large number of Latino/Anusim that are gifted in all areas of construction ranging from residential to commercial, including city and state construction projects. Almost one in every five is a professional in their field.

Over half of them have "some college" education and close to one-third have an undergraduate degree. Approximately one out of every ten has an advanced degree. An increasing number of them are entering highly skilled professions such as medicine, engineering and so forth.

National Patriotism

In terms of patriotism, a large number of men and women serve in every branch of the Armed Forces. They are well represented in the areas of law enforcement, fire departments and rescue teams. Many have won the Medal of Honor for their heroism in combat; and have also incurred a disproportionately high percentage of casualties at war.

Religious and Spiritual Characteristics

The majority of them were brought up as Catholics and their parents or grandparents were Catholic. However, we are discovering that many were what is called, *Catolicos solamente de palabra*. In other words, despite their apparent devout posture, the majority are what I call, "Cultural Catholics."

An increasing number have left the Catholic Church and entered the Evangelical Church system. However, in their recent discovery of their Sephardic Anusim ancestry, there is an exodus from these circles and are engaging in small, private Torah studies with a passion for the Prophets and the prophecies of old. Along with their Jewish cohorts, they strongly anticipate the coming Messiah.

Zionism

The overwhelming majority of them were raised with a deep sense of respect and appreciation for Jews and Israel to the point that they have exited Christian Churches that preach "replacement theology." In other words, they abhor any semblance of faith that despises or minimizes the existence and destiny of Israel, Israelis and Jewish people in general. I have personally heard Latino Anusim young men declare that if they could and were allowed, they would join the IDF (Israeli Defense Forces) to fight against Israel's enemies. There are increasing reports of men and women who volunteer, at their own expense, to assist in the IDF while others volunteer to serve in different kibbutzim.

Summary

For the most part, the Latino Anusim are tenacious, they are not quitters. They are industrious and find ways to make things happen. They are loyal to family and to community. They are "cause oriented." Throughout many generations, they have endured extreme difficulties and leaped over hurdles of gross incompatibility in their lives. They have endured stereotyping as well as subtle racial profiling. In a nutshell, they are survivors. They have learned to live with social injustice just as their forefathers did since the days of Inquisitions past.

It is also true that Latinos, in general, have fought against schemes from outside their camp as well as within them which attempt to divide them. These struggles were maximized throughout the ploys of various Inquisitions which aimed at destroying the Sephardim, whether they were *Marrano conversos* or Sephardic Jews that refused conversion. At any rate, we can yet see fundamental elements of cohesion within the Latino family and community as they continue to prefer serving and assisting one another.

Perhaps, the "miracle" has been that despite being victimized, they have not become like those that have perpetrated against them.

Appendix

Difference between the Holocaust and the Inquisition

There is no difference between a people that suffered at the hand of their perpetrators one year ago as opposed to one decade ago. Pain and suffering was present in both cases. The presence of such trauma did not go away–it remains there as a memorial.

A people that suffered in Hitler's Holocaust 50 years ago is no less and no more than the people that suffered in the Spanish Inquisition 500 years ago. Hitler's fiery ovens were no more and no less than the burnings at the stake of the Inquisitions. The confiscation of goods and property were the same in both cases. The raping of women and girls and even young boys were the same. The kidnappings of their children were no different–a kidnapped child is the same whether it was 50 years ago or 500 years ago. The collective unconscious in both cases is quite similar if not the same. The outcry of the human soul is the same. The demand for justice is exactly the same.

Hitler used Ghettos and Spain used Barrios to hold the Jews under siege. Hitler enforced their wearing a Star of David to distinguish them from all others. Spain used the *San Benito* which was the vesture filled with insane emblems such as snakes and flames to demonstrate who was a Sephardic Jew.

It is nothing short of a miracle we have children of the Holocaust survivors today. It is just as much a miracle, and more so, that we have survivors of the Inquisitions that besieged Spain, Portugal, Mexico, Peru, Columbia, Venezuela, Puerto Rico, Cuba and most Latin American nations including the State of New Mexico in the United States of America.

I wish to God that someone would build a museum of all the atrocities caused upon the Jews of Spain–the Sephardim, the Anusim. There is a major museum of the Holocaust in Jerusalem. In fact, there are more than 20 large and small museums in foreign countries and at least two others in Israel. In our nation there are approximately 25 such museums, the largest one being in Washington, DC. But they have little if any information about the Spanish Inquisition with its tentacles in Iberia and throughout Latin America, and as stated previously also in New Mexico.

I happen to have a dear colleague that deals with the Holocaust survivors in Israel. I personally know a couple of Jewish individuals who are children of Holocaust survivors. I'm glad to report that despite their parent's traumas, they have managed to grow up and make something very special of themselves. But as a mental health professional, I do not need a Sherlock Holmes magnifying glass to detect the effects of their parent's trauma.

On the other hand, I happen to know hundreds and thousands of descendants of the survivors of one or more Inquisitions but their stories are not known. In many cases, they are seen with suspicion and cynicism when they tell a small portion of their forefathers' plight. I am however glad to report that the extended Jewish family is slowly coming around to believe their reports as they become knowledgeable of what actually took place in their histories. But something of a miraculous dimension needs to take place in the halls of the Israeli government in order that these Sephardic Anusim souls be reckoned with in a just and merciful manner.

I am not advocating that any system become gullible to believe anything without proper evidence or due process. But I am declaring that it is high-time that new case law begins to be written along with new policies and procedures that can best deal with such cases. After all, God has given us an amazing tool that is called the brain in order to accurately process intelligence in a wise and prudent manner. But this is going to demand a major amount of change. This means that those that are in positions of power will need to get out of their presumptive boxes in order to hear, see and perceive what is taking place all across the Americas including Iberia and other foreign nations where there are yet Sephardic Anusim Jews in virtual hiding.

It is time for the secular as well as the religious Jews to come together in order to create new pathways that begin to open up, perhaps, small gateways for bona fide cases of Sephardic Anusim. It is time that Israeli politics and religious extremism be put on the shelf until this issue of the awakening of the sleeping giant of Anusim is compatibly dealt with.

In closing, I am convinced we need each other. Sephardic Anusim needs to reconnect with the people as well as the land of their Jewish forefathers. But on the other hand, I'm convinced that Israel needs to stretch out her arms to embrace their orphaned brothers and sisters as they cry out for a little help. Frankly, I shall go out on the limb to declare something very dear to my own heart: Israel needs the Sephardic Anusim more than the Anusim needs Israel because American Anusim are prospering in their American Diaspora.

Most all of the Sephardic Anusim in America that I know, that are longing to make Aliyah are quite resourceful, industrious, loyal and committed Zionists. They may not know half as much about the rudiments and the thousands of years of the Jewish experience. They may not even know what terms such as *Halacha* means neither by definition nor by religious expression, but one thing I do know–they are very teachable. They are pliable and changeable.

The first Prime Minister of Israel, David Ben Gurion stated that if anyone wants to be a Jew, let him. I am sure he wasn't referring to "come one, come all." But I am convinced, after studying his memoirs in the Ben Gurion Heritage Institute in the Negev one summer, I discovered that Ben Gurion knew Israel would need my people, the Sephardic Anusim for times such as now. I have read many of his speeches and public statements and I happen to know that Ben Gurion was a strong believer in the Prophets of the Bible, the Tanakh. His young assistant was once asked by a journalist if Ben Gurion ever sought advice and the young aide said: "Yes, only after he has sought the Prophets."

I therefore, appeal to the powers that be in Israel and the Jewish leaders throughout the globe to take a second and more cautious look at what the holy Prophets have to say about the people I am here advocating for.

Notes

Notes for Introduction

1. DNA test taken under the www.4sephardim.com DNA Project in collaboration with the Family Tree DNA Laboratory in Houston, Texas
2. During a trip to Jerusalem, we found a street which name is similar in pronunciation. I speculated that due to the Spanish and Sephardic Ladino language, *Ancira* may be the combination of two names or a term such as Ben Cira (or Ben Sira). In Hebrew, "Ben" means "son of" and "Cira" or "Sira" would be the name of the father. Thus, when the name *Ancira* would be pronounced in Spanish or Ladino, it could be reduced to *Ancira* rather than *Ben-Cira*. A store owner stated that the name of this street "must have been the name of some famous Jew or hero," but we've not discovered who. We have discovered there is a large Ancira family in Monterrey, Mexico and in San Antonio, Texas among other places in Mexico.
   Additional note: Within the last few days I have finally discovered a few *Ancira* names in a special DNA project of Mexican Jewish origins.
3. Since the term "Sephardic Anusim" is the central theme and is referred to constantly throughout this book there will be instances in which only the term "Anusim" will be used. At other times the term "American Anusim" or "Crypto-Jews" will be used to mean the same thing. The term, "Sephardic" or "Sephardim" means the Jews of Sepharad which is Spain

in the Hebrew language. The term "Anusim" means one that was "forced" or "coerced" to convert from a Jewish lifestyle to Roman Catholicism. The term "Crypto-Jews" refers to hidden Jews or Jews in hiding. It has been said that many Sephardic Anusim have become experts at living as a Catholic by day and a Jew by night.

Notes for Chapter One

4. A few of these experts include: Mordechai Arbell, author of The Jewish Nation of the Caribbean"; Professor Avi Gross of BGU (Ben Gurion University); Professor, Professor Tamar Alexander of the Ladino Center, BGU; Professor Eliezer Papu, BGU; Dr. Chaim Hames, BGU; Ms. Schulamith Chava halevy and many others
5. Deuteronomy 30:4-5, Massoretic Text
6. Jeremiah 32:41 Massoretic Text
7. Obadiah 20b Massoretic Text
8. Isaiah 66:19
9. 1 Kings 9:26; 2 Chronicles 8: 17
10. Zechariah 8: 7, 8
11. Obadiah 20b, Massoretic Text
12. Talmud Shavuous 5a
13. Quotation given to me by Dr. Rabbi Marc D. Angel who is a noted scholar, author of many books on Judaism and Sephardim; and is rabbi emeritus of the Shearith Israel Synagogue in New York City. This was the first synagogue established in North America in 1654 and is also the first Spanish-Portuguese synagogue in the United States
14. Talmud 5a
15. http://en.wikipedia.org/wiki/Talmud

Notes for Chapter Two

16. Sanchez, Dell F. *The Last Exodus*. Jubilee Books. 1998. pp. 4-5
17. 1 Kings 9:26; 2 Chronicles 8: 17

18. The Levites were of the Tribe of Levi and were consecrated for holy priesthood. – The Cohanim were also Levites but were direct descendants of Aaron. In Hebrew, "Cohen" means "minister" of the highest kind.
19. The works of Josephus – complete and unabridged. Hendrickson Publishers, Inc. 1987. pp. 546-7
20. Kagan, Richard L. & Dyer, Abigail. *Inquisitorial Inquiries– brief lives of Secret Jews & Other Heretics.* The Johns Hopkins University Press. 2004. pp. 12, 13
21. Roth, Cecil. *A History of the Marranos.* Jewish Publication Society of America. 1932.
22. Kamen, Henry. *The Spanish Inquisition.* Weidenfeld & Nicolson. 1997. pp. 12-13
23. Gitlitz, David M. *Secrecy and Deceit.* The Jewish Publication Society. 1996. pp. 99-100
24. Hordes, Stanley M. *To the ends of the earth.* Columbia University Press. 2005. pp. 14-15 Op. Cit. Roth. Pp. 2-4; 74-74
25. Op. Cit. Kagan & Dyer. p. 111
26. Op. Cit. Hordes. pp. 30-33
27. Sanchez, Dell F. Aliyah! The Exodus Continues. Authors Choice Press, an Imprint of iUniverse.com. Inc. 2001. p. 26
28. Ibid. p. 28
29. Ibid. pp. 43, 44
30. Heller, Harriet and Fred. Pioneer Jews – A new life in the far west. Houghton Mifflin Co. 1984. p. 2
31. Op. Cit. Hordes. P. 117
32. Quintana, Frances Leon. Pobladores–Hispanic Americans of the Ute Frontier. University of Norte Dame Press. 1991. p. 9
33. Ibid. pp. 133, 136
34. Ibid. pp. 177, 187
35. Some of these customs, practices, traditions and terms are referred to in, Aliyah! The Exodus Continues by Dell F. Sanchez
36. An Israeli Sephardi told a large audience of participants at the International Jewish Genealogy Society conference in Jerusalem, "To many of you, my Spanish is simply Spanish; to me it's Ladino."

37. "Dirty Spanish" was also referred as *impropio y sin cultura* meaning "improper and without culture" when in fact it was a regional dialect of Ladino.
38. Dicionario de la Lengua Española (volumen 1). 1726. Madrid, Spain

Notes for Chapter Three

39. Reference here is to Ruben Duran of Albuquerque, New Mexico in 2004-05
40. Catholic Chapel south of Albuquerque, near La Veguita, New Mexico. 2004/05. In Spanish, "La Veguita" means small water meadows or fertile lands
41. Hordes, Stanley. To the ends of the earth. Columbia University Press. 2005.
42. Campo Santo Rosario. Santa Fe, New Mexico. 2007/8
43. The letters YHVH in Hebrew are יהוה - These letters represent the Holy Name of God which is a transliteration of the four constants forming the Hebrew Tetragrammaton or "incommunicable name" of the Supreme Being, which in latter Jewish tradition is not pronounced save with the vowels of Adonai or Elohim, so that the true pronunciation is lost.
44. San Felipe de Neri Catholic Church constructed in 1793, however, it's been providing services for almost 300 years.
45. This structure is designed in a French Romanesque fashion. While the San Felipe Church is modest in design, St. Francis is quite elegant.
46. Santos, Richard. Silent Heritage—The Sephardim and the Colonization of the Spanish north American frontier, 1492-1600. New Sepharad Press. 2000. pp. 286-287
47. The Mission was designated as a National Historic Landmark on April 15, 1970
48. A *serro* is more of a rugged mountain than an ordinary hill
49. Epigraphy is a type of inscription which literally means, "on-writing." It is the science of identifying the graphemes and of classifying their use as to cultural context and date, elucidating their meaning and assessing what conclusions can be deduced.

50. The Port of Tampico is the place where Don Luis de Carvajal landed his "Santa Catalina" ship filled with Sephardic Crypto-Jews. --The term *Vera Cruz* means "the true cross."
51. This Catholic Convent was named in accordance with Old Spanish as *Combento* rather than its modern version, *Convento*.
52. Op. Cit. Kagan & Dyer. pp. 16-17
53. One Sabbath, as I followed the Torah portion that was being read by the rabbi, to my amazement, I discovered this fact in the commentary at the bottom of the page. These commentaries are written by reputable Jewish sages. Sadly, I did not take note of the Scriptural reference and page number; but am determined to find it in the vast number of pages and commentaries.
54. Villa, Samuel, *Historia de la Inquisición* (History of the Inquisition). Libros CLIE. 1977
55. The term, *garriotiada* was a term frequently used prior to the 1950s-60s by adults of that generation. This term basically meant a person suffering such a whipping felt more like having been mauled in a ruthless manner, almost like a torture.
56. Iron masks were used in order to punish as well as to dehumanize the victims
57. Baer, Yitzhak. *A History of the Jews in Christian Spain*. Volume 2. The Jewish Publication Society. 1992. p.334
58. This torture instrument and caused traumatic humiliation due to the manner it violated human sexual organs

Notes for Chapter Four

59. A "haplogroup" is a formula given to the DNA test results which consists of letters and numbers which identify most ancient as well as recent origins.
60. Family Tree DNA is a commercial genetic genealogy company based in Houston, Texas with its partner laboratory, Arizona Research Labs, housed at the University of Arizona.
61. Ashkenazi Jews are predominantly of Eastern Europe.
62. Kleiman, Yaakov Rabbi. The fascinating story of how DNA studies confirm an ancient biblical tradition. http://www.aish.com/ci/sam/48936742.html

63. Hammer, Bejar, Skorecki, et. al.; Hum Genet (2009) 126:707–717. http://www.springerlink.com/content/357176p177623m41/
64. I have personally witnessed the diversity of physical characteristics among some of these Latinos with a Cohen DNA.
65. This fact was told directly to me by a renowned Jewish expert on DNA

Note for Chapter Five

66. Genesis 2:20 records the first reference to "Adam" which is *aw'dam* in Hebrew. Its Hebrew meaning is "ruddy, flush, rosy," or reddish due to human's thin skin that often reveals bloodlines as opposed to animals with furs or pelts.
67. In Spanish, a surname is known as an *apellido* or *sobrenombre*
68. In Portuguese, this dictionary is called, *Dicionario Sefaradi de Sobrenombres* or Dictionary of Sephardic Surnames.

Notes for Chapter Six

69. It has been confirmed that the surname, Hendrix is directly connected to Enriquez or Henriquez (with a silent H).
70. It must be understood that pronunciation of names and words is always based on one's language and dialect. Therefore, in Spanish, it is very conceivable that the name, "Cohen," took on the enunciation of "Cano" and even "Kano."
71. Leyva or Leiva is the representation of a simple phrase, *Alli va la Ley (there goes the Law)*.
72. "Oral history is the recording, preservation and interpretation of historical information, based on the personal experiences and opinions of the speaker. It often takes the form of eye-witness evidence about past events, but can include folklore, myths, songs and stories passed down over the years by word of mouth." http://en.wikipedia.org/wiki/Oral_history

Bibliography

Spanish Classics

Lisbona, Jose Antonio. *Retorno A Sefarad–La Politica de Espana hacia sus judios en el siglo XX.* Comision nacional Judia Sefarad 92 (Quinto Centenario). 1993

Medina, Joe Toribio. *Historia del Tribunal del Santo Oficio de la Inquisición en Mexico.* UNAM Coordinación de Humanidades. 1987

Toro, Alfonso. *La Familia de Carvajal.* Volumen 1 & 2. Editorial Patria. Mexico DF. 1944

Select Sources in English

Angel, Marc D. Rabbi. *Foundations of Sephardic Spirituality.* Jewish Lights Publishing. 2006

Baer, Yitzhak. *A history of the Jews in Christian Spain.* Volume 1 & 2. The Jewish Publication Society. 1992

Campos, Jacques-Andre Schnieper. *Diccionario de Heraldica.* Editorial LIBSA. 2005

Edwards, John. *The Spanish Inquisition.* Tempus Publishing LTD. 1999

Gitlitz, David M. *Secrecy and Deceit—The Religion of Crypto Jews.* The Jewish Publication Society. 1996

Gubbay, Lucien & Abraham Levy. *The Sephardim.* Carmel Limited. 1992

Hordes, Stanley M. *To the Ends of the Earth.* Columbia University Press. 2005

Kagan, Richard L & Abigail Dyer. *Inquisitorial Inquiries.* The Johns Hopkins University Press. 2004

Kamen, Henry. *The Spanish Inquisition.* The Orion Publishing Group. 1997

Plaidy, Jean. *The Spanish Inquisition.* Barnes & Noble. 1994

Quintana, Frances Leon. *Pobladores–Hispanic Americans of the Ute Frontier.* Norte Dame Press. 1991

Rochlin, Harriet & Fred Rochlin. *Pioneer Jews–A New life in the Far West.* Houghton Mifflin Company. 1984

Roth, Cecil. *History of the Marranos.* The Hebrew Press of the Jewish Publication Society. 1932

Roth, Cecil. *A History of the Jews.* Schocken Books. 1961

Sanchez, Dell F. *The Last Exodus.* Jubilee Books. 1998

Sanchez, Dell F. *Aliyah! The Exodus Continues.* Authors Choice Press. 2001

Sanchez, Dell F. *Sephardic Destiny–A Latino Quest.* Mall Publishing Company. 2003

Sanchez, Dell F. *Obadiah–The Despised Prophet of Sephardim.* Mall Publishing Company. 2004

Santos, Richard G. *Silent Heritage—The Sephardim and the Colonization of the Spanish North American Frontier.* The New Sepharad Press. 2000

About the Author

Dell F. Sanchez was raised in an inner city *barrio* of San Antonio, Texas. He grew with poverty and functional illiteracy all around. Despite socio-economic hardships, he went on to become a university professor in the field of social services/community mental health. He holds a Master of Social Work degree which is accredited by the Council on Social Work Education; a Master of Education degree in counseling psychology; and a Doctor of Philosophy degree in Social Work Education/Administration with a emphasis on Latino community mental health.

Against all odds, he fought for the establishment of a high-power educational television station in his town and succeeded in litigating his case, pro se, in the courts of the Federal Communications Commission. He also orchestrated the construction and operation of the station. He hosted a daily, one hour program named "Jubilee Alive," as well as a Spanish half hour program called *Liberacion*. During this time, he was a member of the National Religious Broadcasters.

He and his wife, Helen, have been tirelessly committed to their quest of awakening Sephardic Anusim who are coming out of their hiding places and letting the world know who they really are. In his passion and within a period of fourteen years he has published nine books, four in English, and four in Spanish and one in German, all on this same subject.

He has conducted conferences and seminars all across America, Mexico, Spain and Switzerland. However, his preferred conference location is in the Negev Desert of Israel. His devotion to his people and to the Negev has led he and his wife to establish a historical exhibit on the Sephardic Anusim of the Americas–how, when and why they got from Israel to Spain and from there into the New World.

In the process, he has developed fruitful relationships with Jewish leaders and rabbis in America and in Israel. He has also managed to open up lines of communication among the Sephardic Anusim–a thing that has been very complex due to the fact that they have been in virtual hiding scattered across tens of thousands of square miles all across the Americas.

He has stated that his highest honor is being embraced by his extended Jewish family and especially by Israeli citizens of all walks of life. It could be said that the overarching theme of his life is how an Israeli colleague once characterized him. She said, "Dell is a fierce Zionist," which portrays him excellently well.

CPSIA information can be obtained at www.ICGtesting.com
227872LV00001B/253-312/P